1984

EYES
OF TEXAS
TRAVEL
GUIDE

Panhandle/Plains Edition

EYES
OF TEXAS
TRAVEL
GUIDE

Panhandle/Plains Edition

Cordovan Corporation, Publishers

Houston 1982

EYES OF TEXAS TRAVEL GUIDE
Panhandle/Plains Edition

Library of Congress Catalog Number: 82-70231
ISBN: 0-89123-024-6
        0-89123-042-4 pbk

Cover photo of Tule Canyon near Lake Mackenzie on Texas Highway 207 by Bill Springer

Cover design: Russell Jumonville
Maps: Kathy Kelley
Production art: Ginny Bliss

This book is dedicated to Jana, Helen, Elizabeth and Veronica.

Ray Miller
Houston
January 1982

Contents

Foreword

I was a small child when I first had the privilege of seeing the Texas Plains. It was in 1923 when our family drove up onto the Caprock of the South Plains east of Lamesa, Texas.

How well do I remember the words my father first spoke when he viewed the unbelievable vastness as we reached the top of the Caprock. He said, "This truly is God's Country."

The flat, level land seemed overwhelmed by more sky than we had ever seen before. The free feeling of space and pure air was unbelievable. Your own eyes determined the view in the distance as there were no barriers.

I was born, grew to the age of twelve in Central Texas near Georgetown. There had been sky in Georgetown, too, but this was a spectacular new world where everything was different.

From its rich, level farmland to its rolling north panhandle ranchland, this area is still glorified in movies, television, plays, books and all media as the land of the cowboys, buffalo, cattle, farms and Indians. Even now, as the last frontier of this great state is growing rapidly, the cowboy spirit of adventure draws thousands here every year to visit or to settle down.

Ray Miller is to be commended for all that he has done that has added so much to our state's history with his *Eyes of Texas Travel Guides*. I am especially happy that he is publishing this Panhandle Plains Edition, the story of our last colorful frontier.

Preston Smith
Governor of Texas 1969-73

The Plains of West Texas are of two varieties. The High Plains are almost as flat as a table. The Rolling Plains, here, are a little less high and a lot less flat.

Introduction

This sixth volume completes the EYES OF TEXAS TRAVEL GUIDE series. The PANHANDLE/PLAINS EDITION deals with the 52 counties in the northwest corner of the state. The area includes all of the Panhandle and most of the Texas High Plain also known as the Llano Estacado.

Texans claimed territory far beyond the present north and west boundaries of the state when they established the republic in 1836. But few Anglo Texans took any interest in the area that is now the Panhandle until 40 years later. It was Indian country. The Apaches the Spanish found here in the sixteenth century had been crowded out by the Comanches and Kiowas from the Northern Plains by the time the Republic of Texas was established. Hundreds of thousands of buffalo grazed here then. The whole area was covered with tall grass. But there was little surface water and the early explorers mistakenly thought it was part of the Great American Desert.

Cowmen discovered the underground water in the 1870s. Windmills sprouted on the Plains in the 1880s. Irrigation began in a small way in the 1890s.

Hundreds of thousands of acres of rangeland have been converted to agriculture since then. Plains farmers raise staggering crops of cotton, wheat, corn, sorghum and vegetables with the water from the vast Ogallala Aquifer. But the aquifer is not the inexhaustible reservoir the farmers once thought it was. The water table is dropping. Some experts believe the acreage under irrigation will have to be reduced drastically by 2020. Some farmland already is being converted back to pasture. More will be. But in 1982 it is still possible for Plains farmers to pump enough water to produce crops big enough to drive prices down below the point where the farmers can break even.

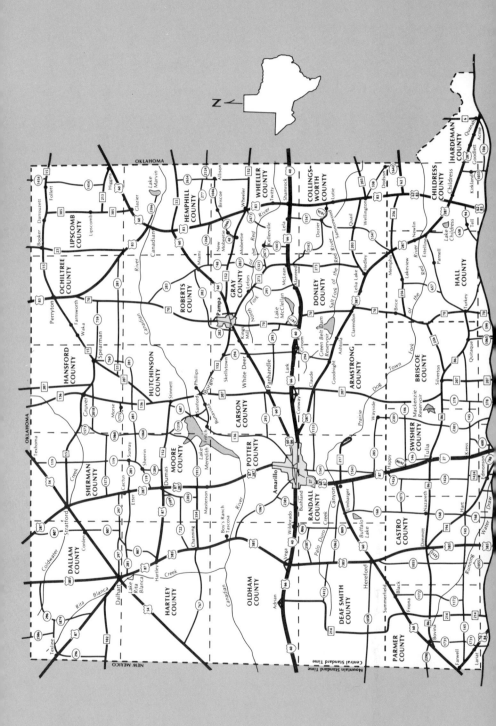

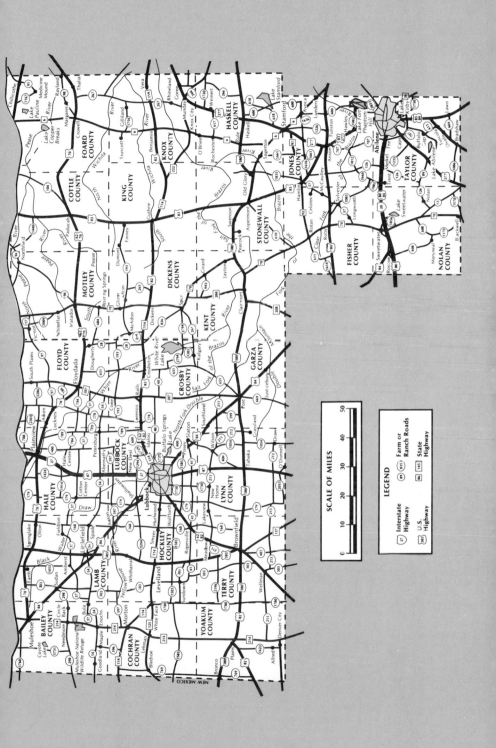

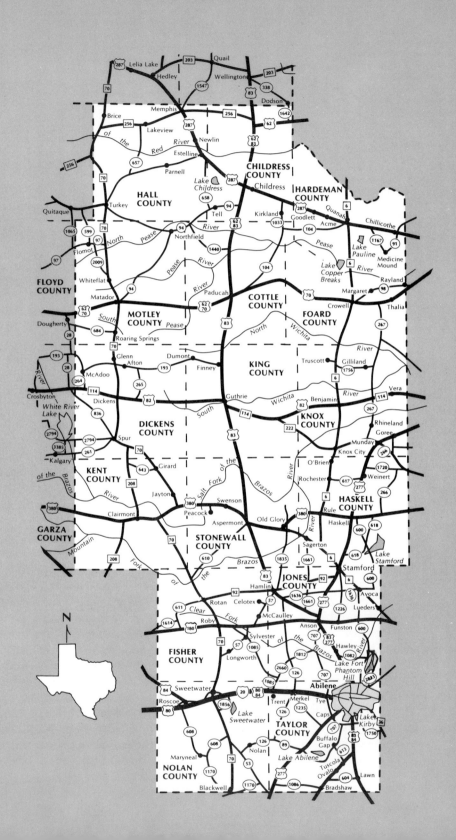

Abilene and the Rolling Plains

*Taylor, Nolan, Fisher, Jones, Haskell,
Stonewall, Kent, Dickens, King, Knox,
Foard, Cottle, Motley, Hall, Childress and
Hardeman counties.*

The High Plains of Texas are the southern end of the Great High Plains that lie east of the Rocky Mountains all the way from Canada to Texas. The Rolling Plains of Texas are the southern end of the Great Plains of North America. The boundary between the High Plains and the Rolling Plains in Texas is the escarpment known as the Cap Rock. The High Plains are monotonously flat. There are gentle hills and valleys on the Rolling Plains.

Almost all of the Panhandle-Plains area was included in the original Bexar District by the first Congress of the Republic of Texas. Most of the present 52 counties were created by the legislature in 1876 at the end of the Reconstruction Period. There was little serious attempt to settle whites here before that because of the Indians. But the legislature did create five counties here in 1858. They were Hardeman, Knox, Haskell, Jones and Taylor. The other four were re-created in 1876. The only county here dating from 1858 is Taylor County.

1

2

1) Before there was Abilene there was Buffalo Gap. This was the first settlement in Taylor County and the original county seat. The original court house square is now privately owned but it is open to the public for a fee. The stone building in the background is the original jail. It was built in 1880.
2) The county government moved to Abilene but people still live in Buffalo Gap and a lot of former residents come back for the Old Settlers' Reunion in July. The old town has several antique stores and souvenir shops.
3) Lake Abilene provides water for Abilene and sport for fishermen. The lake is off Farm Road 89 southwest of Buffalo Gap.

3

TAYLOR COUNTY

This county was named for one of the families the empresario Sterling Clack Robertson brought to Texas in the 1830s. It was on the edge of civilization when the legislature created it in 1858. Fort Belknap had been built in Young County to the northeast seven years earlier. Fort Chadbourne had been built in Coke County to the southwest six years earlier as the U.S. Army extended the chain of frontier outposts it started at Fort Worth in 1849. The road connecting Belknap and Chadbourne was the road the early Butterfield stagecoaches used. It came right through Taylor County.

There is a line of hills called the Callahan Divide separating the Brazos River watershed and the Colorado River watershed. This line of hills is the southern boundary of the Rolling Plains and the northern boundary of the Edwards Plateau.

1) *Abilene State Recreation Area has provisions for camping, swimming and hiking. The number for reservations is 915-572-3204.*

2) *Military and civilian groups are developing a military museum at Dyess Air Force Base to include this WWII bomber and other exhibits. The base was established in 1956 and named for WWII hero William Dyess of Albany, Texas.*

1

B-17 FLYING FORTRESS
DEDICATED TO THE MEMORY OF
THE MEMBERS OF THE 96TH BOMB GROUP
AND THE 96TH BOMB WING WHO HAVE GIVEN
THEIR LIVES IN SERVICE OF THEIR COUNTRY.
AND PRESENTED TO THE CITY OF ABILENE
BY THE 96TH BOMB GROUP ASSOCIATION.

2

There is a break in these hills near the center of Taylor County. The buffalo used this pass to avoid climbing the hills during their migrations. The pass therefore was a favorite Indian campground for generations. White buffalo hunters haunted the place after they began the systematic slaughter of the buffalo. They called it Buffalo Gap.

The Butterfield stages and all the military traffic between the forts came through Buffalo Gap. It was a natural place for a settlement. And the settlement that grew up at Buffalo Gap was a natural place for the county seat in 1878 when there finally were enough people in the county to organize a government.

Buffalo Gap had twelve hundred people, several saloons and a stone jail by 1880. But the county government moved away that year to a new town on the new railroad line in the northeast corner of the county. The new town was named

1

1) Abilene Christian University is supported by the Church of Christ. It started as a prep school in 1906. It became a junior college in 1914 and a senior college in 1919 and a university in 1976. This is the Moody Coliseum on the A.C.U. campus.

2) This gun on the Hardin-Simmons University campus in Abilene is a memorial to students and graduates killed in WWI. The school was Simmons College at that time. It was founded in 1891. Hardin was added to the name in 1934 after oilman John G. Hardin made a big donation. This Baptist school is the home of the Hardin-Simmons Cowboy Band.

3) The Methodists founded McMurry College in 1923 and named it for a former bishop.

2

3

MC MURRY
COLLEGE

1) Abilene's striking courthouse was built in 1971. Taylor County was named for three pioneer brothers. Edward, James and George Taylor settled in the Robertson Colony in south central Texas.

2) There is no railroad passenger service here anymore. The T&P depot is now a freight office for the Missouri Pacific. The Hotel Drake is abandoned. The tall building in the background was the Wooten Hotel. It is a retirement home, now. The businesses have moved to suburban malls.

1

2

3) The Abilene Fine Arts Museum is open every day except Monday. It is on the southside in the Oscar Rose Park on Mockingbird.

4) Will Hair Park is near the site of the old Hashknife Ranch headquarters where ranchers and railroad men met to pick the site for Abilene.

3   4

Abilene today is a prosperous and modern city. There is a replica of what the town may have looked like in the late 1880s on IH-20 northeast of the city. Old Abilene Town has many authentic artifacts and antiques. There is a fee, but overnight trailer parking is free.

Abilene. A place named Abilene is mentioned in the Bible, in the third chapter of Luke. But the ranchers collaborating with the railroad in founding it chose the name of this town. And their inspiration was the cowtown in Kansas.

The same year Abilene was established, the citizens petitioned for an election to move the county seat. The residents of Buffalo Gap put on a spirited campaign to keep the government. They lost. They said it was because a lot of passengers voted illegally while they were passing through Abilene on the trains. There was some legal skirmishing but the government moved to Abilene. It has been in Abilene ever since and Abilene has been growing almost ever since. It is the most important city on the Rolling Plains with a big Air Force base, two universities, a college and several factories. Buffalo Gap eventually got rail service, too, but it never grew much.

The Ogallala Aquifer does not extend to Taylor County. Rainfall averages around 23 inches. There is some farming. Cotton and grains are the principal crops. But ranching is bigger than farming in Taylor County. Oil was discovered in 1929 but Taylor County is not one of the really big oil producers.

1

2

1) A number of small animals and several large ones are on exhibit in the zoo in Nelson Park opposite the County Stadium on South 11th.

2) The city and county and various businessmen put up money to drill a demonstration oil well on the County Stadium grounds for the Abilene Centennial in 1981. They claimed to be surprised when they hit oil.

3) This suburb on the outskirts of Abilene voted to incorporate and allow liquor in 1960 when all the surrounding area was dry. Pinkie's store did a huge business. Abilene voted wet in 1978. The monopoly ended and this store closed but Pinkie's is still in business elsewhere.

3

NOLAN COUNTY

This county also is on the line between the Rolling Plains and the Edwards Plateau. Nolan County was created in 1876 from parts of the Bexar and Young districts. It was named for the man said to have been the first Anglo to make a map of Texas. Philip Nolan was born in Ireland. He settled in Kentucky in 1788 but he spent most of his time in Texas after 1790. Nolan made at least four expeditions from Nacogdoches into the interior of Spanish Texas. His ostensible purpose was to round up wild horses for buyers in Louisiana. But the Spanish thought Nolan was a U.S. agent and they killed him when they caught up with him in central Texas in 1801.

There were no settlers in Nolan County when it was created. There were only a few cattle camps and a few buffalo hunters. Buffalo skins were in great demand in the East and in Europe in the 1870s. White buffalo hunters swarmed onto the Texas Plains to fill this demand. They slaughtered the buffalo and took the skins and left the rest of the animals where they fell. The slaughter appalled the Plains Indians.

A branch of the Texas State Technical Institute and the Sweetwater Municipal Airport now occupy the site of a WWII air base, northwest of Sweetwater. Not much is left except this old hangar from the days when this was Avenger Field. Pilots were trained here for Britain's Royal Air Force and for our Army Air Corps between 1942 and 1943. Avenger Field was devoted after April of 1943 to training pilots for the U.S. Women's Airforce Service Pilots (WASP). More than 1,000 women qualified here to fly military planes on all kinds of missions except combat missions.

They were supposedly confined to the reservations in Oklahoma by this time. But they lived to hunt buffalo and they had been promised in the Medicine Lodge Treaty in 1867 that they would have exclusive rights to hunt on these Plains. The U.S. government, though, made a promise in that treaty it had no real right to make. Vacant lands in Texas belonged to the state under the Treaty of Annexation and the U.S. had no jurisdiction. The Texas legislature considered a bill to stop the slaughter but General Philip Sheridan headed it off by explaining to the lawmakers that killing off the buffalo was the best way to get the Indians off the Plains. The slaughter continued and much of the mischief perpetrated by the Comanches and Kiowas in the middle 1870s was in retaliation.

The buffalo hunters in Nolan County and the Indians before them made a habit of camping on Sweetwater Creek. It was a place where they found water they could drink. There were not many such places in the area. Much of the water here

1

2

1) The Pioneer City-County Museum in Sweetwater is housed in a home lawyer R.A. Ragland built in 1906 at East 3rd and Ragland.

2) The museum has ten rooms full of art and artifacts and photographs from the early days. It is open afternoons except Mondays. There is no charge for admission.

3) A limestone office building R.A. Ragland built in 1901 still stands on the courthouse square in Sweetwater. Another law firm has its offices here now and there is a restaurant on the ground floor. The old Ragland Building is listed in the **National Register of Historic Places.**

3

tastes of gypsum.

A trader named Tom Knight opened a store for the buffalo hunters in a dugout on the bank of Sweetwater Creek about 1877. A little settlement grew up and a post office was established in 1879. The settlement by that time was being called Sweetwater. The settlement was designated the county seat when the county was organized in 1881. Sweetwater moved two miles to the northwest a little later the same year to get on the rail line the Texas and Pacific was extending toward El Paso.

Sweetwater had a few rough years. The town was incorporated in 1884 but the residents let the corporation lapse in 1885 because money was so scarce. The corporation was revived in 1897 and Sweetwater became an important railroad town. It is an important marketing and manufacturing center today served by Interstate Highway 20.

Almost seventy-five percent of the population of Nolan County is concentrated in Sweetwater. Most of the rest of the

1

2

1) *Nolan County's sleek pink granite courthouse was built in 1977 to replace a 1918 model.*
2) *Travelers camp in the trailer park at Sweetwater Lake for $2.50 a night.*
3) *The name Sweetwater celebrates the fact that there is some water here that does not have gypsum in it. But the gypsum has its uses. U.S. Gypsum Company has been making sheetrock at a big plant outside Sweetwater since 1923. Flintkote makes a similar wallboard at a plant nearby. (U.S. Gypsum owns the name Sheetrock.) These plants heat and treat the gyp rock until it is a paste and then press it into boards between sheets of paper.*

3

county is in farms and ranches. But the oil and gas fields and the deposits of lime, gravel and gypsum earn more money than the farms and ranches. The oil was discovered in 1939.

The big event in Sweetwater is the annual Rattlesnake Roundup with prizes for the people bringing in the most and biggest live snakes. This is held the second weekend in March. There is a gun show and usually a flea market along with the Rattlesnake Roundup.

Fisher County tore down a courthouse built in the early 1900s to put up this building in Roby in 1973. It looks more like a clinic than a courthouse.

FISHER COUNTY

This county was named for the first Texas Navy Secretary. The original Texas Navy consisted of four secondhand schooners purchased by the General Council of the provisional government in January of 1836, before the Declaration of Independence. The ships saw a little action in the Gulf of Mexico under the command of Commodore Charles Hawkins during the revolution.

Sam Houston appointed Samuel Rhoads Fisher to be secretary of the navy when he became president of the republic in October of 1836. Fisher had come to Texas from Pennsylvania in 1830. He was one of the signers of the Texas Declaration of Independence. The navy was down to one ship when Fisher was named secretary. Only the schooner *Independence* was operating. A shipyard in New Orleans had seized and sold the *Liberty* because Texas couldn't pay for repairs the shipyard had made. The *Brutus* and *Invincible* were in New York for repairs and they would have been seized and sold if Samuel Swartwout had not advanced the money to pay the shipyard bill. Swartwout was U.S. Collector of Customs for the Port of New York at the time and he was dabbling in Texas real estate on the side.

The Mexicans captured the *Independence* early in 1837. But the *Brutus* and *Invincible* were back in Texas waters by then. Secretary Fisher decided he should go on a little cruise with his navy. He said it would improve the crews' morale. President Houston disapproved. He wanted the navy to stay close to the coast. But Fisher did it his way. He took the *Brutus* and *Invincible* out for a couple of months and attacked some Mexican ships and raided some Mexican villages. He lost the *Invincible* on a sandbar off Galveston during a skirmish with

1

2

1) *The Fisher County Courthouse is different from the usual Texas court-house in being built around an atrium. Courtrooms and offices are all on the same floor, on corridors opening off this garden room.*
2) *One of the places recognized by the* **National Register of Historic Places** *as having been inhabited by humans 10,000 years ago is the Steadman site in southeast Fisher County. It's private, owned by Link Adair.*

Mexican ships in August of 1837. A storm destroyed the *Brutus* in October of the same year.

President Houston fired Fisher. He claimed the navy secretary had been using the navy's ships for smuggling. The Texas Senate cleared Fisher of that charge. But all the Texas Navy's ships were gone. The Republic was without a navy until early 1839 when it started buying some more ships. Samuel Rhoads Fisher was gone by that time. He died in March of 1839 at the age of 45.

The legislature named this county for Secretary Fisher when it was created in 1876. There were very few people here then. The first census was in 1880 and it showed a population of 136 for the entire county. Four of the residents listed farming as their occupation. All the others were cattlemen or cowboys. Farmers were encouraged by the occasional wet cycles on the Plains and wiped out by the dry cycles. There were many small farms in this area in the 1920s and '30s and the population of the county reached a peak of almost 13,000 in 1940. There are few small farms left today. The successful agricultural enterprises on the Plains are the ranches and feedlots and big mechanized farms.

Farming and ranching produce about one-third of the income in Fisher County. The rest comes from the oil and gas and gypsum. The oil was discovered in 1928.

High school football is a passion on the Texas Plains. Almost everybody in towns like Hamlin goes to the Friday night games. Coach Bill Grissom here is drilling his Hamlin Pied Pipers for the 1981 regional championship game the Pipers won the following night. A good part of the town of Hamlin is in Jones County. Hamlin High School has students from both Fisher and Jones counties.

The town of Roby was designated the county seat when Fisher County was formally organized in 1886. The town was named for landowners D. C. and M. L. Roby. The population of Roby is less than 700. Rotan and Hamlin both are larger. But Hamlin is partly in Jones County.

JONES COUNTY

This county and the county seat both were named for the last president of the Republic of Texas. Dr. Anson Jones was elected president in 1844 and he served until Texas formally became a state in 1846. Jones was born in Massachusetts. He came to Texas in 1833 and started practicing medicine in Brazoria. He served in the Texas Army during the revolution and he was a member of the second Congress of the Republic. He was minister to the United States and secretary of state at different times under President Houston. Jones always claimed he deserved more credit than Houston was willing to allow him for the policies that led to Texas being annexed to the United States. He was very critical of Houston and some of the other early movers and shakers in his book, *Republic of Texas*, published after he killed himself in 1858.

Jones County was created by the legislature originally in 1858. It was re-created in 1876 when most of the other counties in this end of the state were being created. John Merchant started the settlement that became the town of Anson before the state started offering land here for sale. Merchant was guessing that the Texas and Pacific Railroad was going to build its line through Jones County. He staked a claim to a

1

2

1) *A couple of small stone buildings still stand but most of old Fort Phantom Hill was destroyed by fire years ago. The site is covered with mesquite trees and prickly pears and a few stone chimneys. This is private property but the owner tolerates sightseers. The ruins are right on Farm Road 600 north of Abilene. The site is a National Historic Landmark.*

2) *There is a free boat ramp and picnic area on Lake Fort Phantom Hill just south of the ruined fort. No overnight camping is allowed at this spot but campsites are available at marinas around the lake. Lake Fort Phantom Hill furnishes water for the city of Abilene.*

tract of land in the middle of the county. He built a corral for the convenience of the ranchers and he offered to put up buildings for settlers willing to start businesses in what he was calling Jones City. McD Bowyer agreed to open a store and P. S. Tipton agreed to start a hotel. Both men stayed and eventually bought from the state the sites they occupied. But John Merchant moved on to Taylor County as soon as he found out that the T&P was going to build there instead of through Jones County. Jones City had a population of 14 when the county government was organized in 1881. There was an election to choose a permanent county seat and Jones City won. The residents of the new county seat changed the name of their town the following year to Anson.

Hotelman M. H. Rhodes staged a Christmas ball at his Morning Star Hotel in Anson in 1885. It became an annual affair and it got national attention after Larry Chittenden wrote his poem in 1892 about the *Cowboys' Christmas Ball.*

The Jones County government had its seat briefly at Fort

1   2

1) A statue of the last president of the Republic of Texas sits in front of the Jones County Courthouse in Anson. The county and the county seat were named for Dr. Anson Jones. The courthouse was built in 1910. The Cowboys Christmas Ball is still held here in Anson every December as it has been since 1885.

2) Some of the early Texas opera houses have been restored. This one on the town square in Anson has not. The Anson Opera House was built in 1907. The historical marker says the first Anson High School graduation exercise was held here in 1909. A variety store occupies the ground floor. One of the letters is missing from the name. It should be "Spot Cash."

Phantom Hill before the election was held to fix a permanent county seat. The fort had been abandoned years earlier, but there was a small settlement still at the site in 1881. The U.S. Army had established the fort on a hill in the southeast corner of what is now Jones County in 1851. It was one of the outposts in the original chain of forts on the Indian frontier. Some of the soldiers came back and set the buildings on fire after the army abandoned the post in 1854. It never had been a popular duty station. It was a long way from anywhere and even the drinking water had to be hauled in. The fort had no name during the time the Army was using it. It began to be called Phantom Hill after the army left.

The Texas and Pacific line missed Jones County. But the Texas Central Railroad laid tracks across the north end of the county when it extended its line from Albany to Rotan in 1899. The Texas Central established some new towns along the way because that was one of the more profitable prerogatives of the railroad builders. The Texas Central established Stamford. It was named for the railroad president's hometown in Connecticut. Ranchers in the area northwest of the new town raised a big subsidy to promote a rail line between Stamford and Spur and Stamford became an important town. It is still the biggest town in the county.

1

2

1) Stamford is about twice as big as Anson. Stamford has never been the county seat but the town has some of the atmosphere of a county seat. The business district is grouped around a square. But the building occupying the square is not a courthouse. This is the U.S. Post Office. It has been here since 1917. Also on the square is the Stamford Cowboy Country Museum. It is open weekdays and there is no admission fee. The museum is on the east side of the square, behind the post office. 2) The Texas Cowboy Reunion has been held here for the past 52 years. The Texas Cowboy Reunion Rodeo bills itself as the greatest amateur rodeo in the world. Three hundred and forty-eight contestants entered the 1981 event. The rodeo is staged at the Reunion grounds on the west side of Stamford. The Reunion always coincides with the July Fourth holidays. The program includes old time fiddling contests, displays of western art and chuckwagon meals on the Reunion grounds, besides the rodeo.

Oldtimers in Stamford organized the Texas Cowboy Reunion in 1930 to preserve some of the traditions and customs of the Old West. The Texas Cowboy Reunion Rodeo draws people from all over the country to the Reunion grounds on the western outskirts of Stamford. The Cowboy Reunion is held every summer during the July Fourth holidays.

Oil was discovered in Jones County in 1926. But agriculture produces more income here than the oil and gas. Farming is bigger than ranching now. The big crops are cotton, feed grains and wheat.

A big stone marker at the intersection of State Highway 283 and U.S. 277 north of Stamford recalls that Colonel Ranald Mackenzie came this way in 1874 enroute to his showdown with Quanah Parker and the Quahadi Comanches.

HASKELL COUNTY

This is another one of the counties the Texas legislature first created in 1858 and then re-created in 1876 because nothing much happened after the first creation. Captain Randolph Marcy and his troops came through here when they were scouting trails for the California emigrants in 1849. They found a couple of reliable water holes. Some of the emigrants following the Marcy Trail later wrote favorable accounts back to relatives in the east. One small group came here in 1855 planning to settle. But they gave the idea up because of the Indians' attitude. The Comanches and the Kiowas still were emphatically of the opinion that this was their exclusive domain.

White buffalo hunters were in the area by the middle 1870s. The Reynolds and Matthews Cattle Company established a cow camp in the county in 1879 and T. F. Tucker started the first settlement about the same time. Tucker settled beside a spring in the middle of the county. He named the place Rice Springs for one of the employees of the Reynolds and Matthews outfit. A couple more families settled at Rice Springs in 1883. The first store opened in 1884. Rice Springs was the only settlement in Haskell County when the county government was organized in 1885 so it was designated the county seat. T. F. Tucker was elected county judge and the name of the town was changed. The settlers decided to give their town the same name the legislature had given the county.

The name Haskell honors the memory of one of the Texas soldiers the Mexicans executed at Goliad. Charles Ready Haskell was not a Texas settler. He was just eighteen and still

1) Haskell County's limestone courthouse was built in Haskell in 1931. Travelers will notice that the people on the Plains have an overwhelming preference for cars and trucks made in the USA.

2) The Wichita Valley Railroad extended a line into Haskell County in 1906 and built this depot in Haskell. Passenger service ended in 1951. The old depot has been a museum since 1960. It is in the city park. The original furnishings are still inside. Travelers with trailers or RVs can camp free overnight in this little park.

3) The Anchor Marina in Haskell County's Scott Park on the north shore of Lake Stamford has a free boat ramp. The concessionaire collects a fee for camping and picnicking. The park is off Farm Road 618. The lake supplies water for Stamford and other towns.

in school in Tennessee when he heard that there was fighting in Texas. The Texans were offering free land to any volunteers willing to help them. Haskell and many other young Americans hurried to Texas to get in on the action.

Haskell enlisted at Nacogdoches in a company commanded by Captain B. L. Lawrence. He was later transferred to Captain Burr Duval's company. Duval had arrived from Kentucky with a party of volunteers in November of 1835. Haskell went with Duval's company to Goliad to reinforce Colonel James Fannin's garrison. Fannin's little army was intercepted by the Mexicans as it tried to retreat from Goliad in March of 1836 after the Alamo fell. Fannin made a stand at Coleto Creek and then surrendered. The Mexicans took the Texans back to Goliad and executed them a week later in what Texans ever since have referred to as the Goliad Massacre. Counties were named also for Fannin and Duval.

Haskell County has been producing oil and gas since 1929 but it is not one of the big oil producers. Agriculture here accounts for almost twice as much of the county's income as oil does. There is some ranching, but the cotton and grain crops are the biggest money-makers in Haskell County.

2) The first county seat in Stonewall County was Rayner. Nothing is left except the courthouse and it has been a private residence since 1915. The old courthouse is off U.S. 380, 7½ miles east of Aspermont.

1) The first settlement in Stonewall County was a trading post on the Double Mountain Fork of the Brazos River in the southern part of the present county. The settlers were all buffalo hunters and hide traders and they only stayed as long as the buffalo lasted. Occasionally the hunters took a buffalo tongue or a hump for the table but most of the meat was left to rot during the great buffalo slaughter of the 1870s.

STONEWALL COUNTY

The first great market place for buffalo hides when the real slaughter of the buffalo began in the early 1870s was Dodge City in Kansas. The trade in hides inspired a few free enterprisers to push out into the Indian country to sell supplies to the buffalo hunters and buy their hides from them. One of these hide traders was Charles Rath. He set up camp first in the Texas Panhandle near the new Fort Elliott in Wheeler County. Rath and two partners moved on down in 1876 to the bank of the Double Mountain Fork of the Brazos River in Stonewall County. Here they set up a camp they called Rath City. This was such a precarious location that the army sent two dozen soldiers out from Fort Griffin to live at the camp and protect the traders from the Indians.

Rath and company sold powder and whiskey and lead and other supplies to the buffalo hunters and bought buffalo hides by the wagon load. Rath's big wagons hauled the hides to Dodge City and brought back more supplies. Rath City was a busy place for about two years until most of the buffalo had been killed. Rath and his partners moved to the Indian Territory then and opened a trading post at Fort Supply.

1   2

*1) The Stonewall County government moved from Rayner to Aspermont in
1898. The present brick courthouse was built in 1911. Aspermont has not
been growing in recent years. Almost half the business buildings on the
courthouse square are abandoned. The mall builders have not reached
Aspermont, yet.*
*2) Stonewall County was named for Confederate General Thomas J.
Jackson. He was not a Texan but General Barnard Bee of Texas first called
him "Stonewall" because of his stubborn refusal to yield ground to Union
troops at the first battle of Manassas.*

The legislature created this county in 1876 and named it for
General Thomas J. Jackson. He was one of the chief heroes
of the Confederacy better known as "Stonewall" Jackson.
The first cattlemen moved into the area in 1877. The first
settler was Dennis Hodges. He settled near the present town
of Aspermont in the early 1880s.

The first county government was organized in 1888. A little
settlement on the W. E. Rayner ranch in the eastern part of
the county was chosen to be the county seat. But there was
another election in 1890 and the voters decided to move the
county seat to Aspermont, near the center of the county. The
residents of Rayner contested the election and the move was
delayed until 1898. Aspermont has been the county seat since
then.

Aspermont was not one of the towns blessed with early rail
service. The Stamford and Northwestern Railroad did not
reach here until 1909. Travel between Aspermont and Stamford before that was by stage.

There was some excitement in Stonewall County in 1900
when a man named Echols claimed he had found a silver mine
in a canyon northeast of town. Echols offered stock for sale.
He subdivided his property and sold off lots in what he said
was going to be a new mining town. A couple of thousand

1) *The Double Mountain Fork of the Brazos River takes its name from this modest set of hills in the southwest corner of Stonewall County. Double Mountain is only 2,300 feet at its highest point.*
2) *This town was called New Brandenberg when it was founded in 1903. The original settlers were Germans but the name became an embarrassment during WWI and the residents petitioned to get the name changed to something more American.*

people were taken before they found out they were being taken. They discovered after Echols took off with their money that the "mine" had been salted with silver from somewhere else. There never was any silver mined in Stonewall County.

One of the early ranchers in this area was Swen M. Swenson. His S M S Ranches operated in Kent and Jones and Throckmorton counties and near Flattop here in Stonewall County. Swenson was said to have been the first Swedish immigrant to settle in Texas. He and his uncle, Svante Palm, helped several hundred other Swedes move to this state. The town of Swenson in western Stonewall County was named for Swen Swenson.

Oil was discovered here in 1938. There is substantial production and the income from the oil and gas and gypsum is several times what the farms and ranches in Stonewall County earn.

KENT COUNTY

This county has a lot of oil and more cows than people. The oil was not discovered here until 1946 but only about thirty counties in the state now produce more than Kent County. There is some farming here but most of the land is in ranches and livestock produces about twice as much income as the farm crops.

About 1,200 people live in Kent County and more than half of them live in Jayton on the eastern edge of the county. Jayton is not an old town. It was founded in 1909 when the

1

2   3

1) This is another county where the government moved away from the original county seat. The old Kent County Courthouse in Clairemont is still used occasionally as a meeting hall and voting place. This courthouse was built in 1893.

2) Old Clairemont is almost deserted. These once were business buildings on the town square. The only business left is one combination store and filling station.

3) The old jail building stands open, inviting vandals. The county government left here for Jayton in 1954.

first railroad came through. The railroad was the one the Plains ranchers had promoted to connect Stamford and Spur. It was originally called the Stamford and Northwestern and later became part of the Wichita Valley Line. Jayton was named for the owners of the land the town was built on.

Ranald Mackenzie's troops fought one of their battles with the Comanches in what is now Kent County in 1872. Buffalo hunters moved in after that but there were no settlers here when the legislature created the county in 1876. Cattlemen moved in first and R. L. Rhomberg arrived in 1888. Rhomberg established a settlement in the center of the county and named it for his daughter Claire. Clairemont became the county seat when the county government was organized in 1892. But Clairemont never grew very much. It never got rail

1

1) *The present Kent County Courthouse in Jayton was built when the government moved here from Clairemont in 1954. A marker on the courthouse lawn asserts that the northernmost business activity in Texas during the Civil War was a plant producing salt from a spring that feeds into the Salt Fork of the Brazos River.*

2) *Artists and writers interested in the American West frequented a resort in Putoff Canyon off Croton Creek just north of Jayton in the early 1900s. Zane Grey used this area as the setting for his book* **The Thundering Herd.** *The canyon was named for a man named Putoff.*

2

service. The population never reached much more than 200.

The Kent County voters decided at an election in 1952 to move the county seat to the bigger town of Jayton. A legal battle delayed the move. But the government did move to Jayton in 1954 and Clairemont became a ghost town.

Kent County was named for one of the men killed at the Alamo in 1836. Andrew Kent had come to Texas in 1828 probably from Missouri but maybe from Pennsylvania. He settled on the Lavaca River. He was living in Gonzales when the revolution against Mexico started. Kent and 31 other men of Gonzales answered William Barret Travis' plea for reinforcements when the Mexican army started its siege of the Alamo. They marched to San Antonio and joined the Alamo garrison in time to be killed with Travis and all the others on March 6th. Texas history books often refer to the men from Gonzales as the "Immortal 32." They were the only reinforcements to reach the Alamo before the fall.

DICKENS COUNTY

Most of this county is on the Rolling Plains. But the High Plains reach into the northwest corner of Dickens County. The town of McAdoo is on the high plain. All the other towns in the county are on the Rolling Plains. U.S. Highway

1   2

1) The size has been reduced considerably and the ownership has changed several times but the old Spur Ranch is still in business here in Dickens County.

2) Part of the original Spur Ranch is now the town of Spur. This is the biggest town in the county. The museum here grew out of the collection of prehistoric artifacts Bill Elliot found while he was working on the Spur Ranch. Elliot left his collection to his daughter Margaret and she donated it to the citizens of Spur. The Margaret A. Elliot Museum is open Monday, Tuesday, Wednesday, Thursday and Saturday afternoons. Spur was another place popular with western artists and writers in the early 1900s.

82 crosses the Cap Rock escarpment a few miles west of Dickens. Dickens is the county seat. The town and the county were named for J. Dickens. He was one of the defenders of the Alamo.

This was Comanche territory until the middle 1870s. Colonel Ranald Mackenzie had a supply base here during the final U.S. Army campaign against the Comanches and Kiowas in 1874 and 1875. The base was called Anderson's Fort because it was commanded by Major Thomas Anderson. It was on a small flat-topped mountain south of the present town of Dickens. The mountain is labeled Soldiers Mound on today's maps. Mackenzie's troops re-grouped here following their engagements with the Indians in Tule Canyon and Palo Duro Canyon. Several soldiers were buried on Soldiers Mound. The army abandoned the base in January of 1875.

Cattlemen moved into the area as the soldiers left. The Pitchfork, Matador and Spur ranches ran cattle here before the first settlers arrived. The Spur Ranch was bought and sold several times before 1907. It was subdivided that year. The owners established the town of Spur on part of the propety and helped promote the extension of the rail line from Stamford. The rail line reached Spur in 1909 and Spur has been the biggest town in the county almost ever since.

The legislature created Dickens County in 1876. The county

1

2

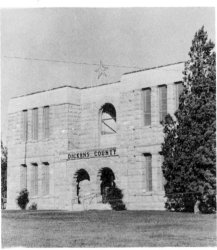

3

1) The U.S. Army had a base camp on Soldiers' Mound south of the present town of Dickens during the campaign against the Comanches. It was called a fort but there were no permanent buildings, only sandbags.
2) The Dickens County Museum is housed in an old store building on the courthouse square in Dickens. Some of them are very small, like this one, but most counties now have museums. They tend to grow as old-timers realize there is a place for the relics their children regard as junk.
3) The Dickens County Courthouse is one of the old ones. This building was put up in 1893. The tower and gables were lopped off during a remodeling in 1936. The population of Dickens is under 300.

had one store, one post office, one school, three houses and 28 people in 1880. Most of the residents were cowboys working for the big ranches. Settlement began at what is now the town of Dickens in the middle 1880s and Dickens was chosen to be the county seat when the government was organized in 1891.

The Spur Ranch started doing a little experimental farming in the early 1880s. Homesteaders were encouraged by a few fairly wet years to plant crops. Many of these small farmers were wiped out by drought in the late 1880s and forced to go to work on the ranches. The number of small farms increased gradually, though, until around 1940. The trend has been toward fewer and bigger farms since then. This has also been the case on the Plains, generally. The 1950 census showed a population of 7,139 for Dickens County. The present population is about half that figure. Cattle, cotton and wheat produce most of the income here. Oil was discovered in 1953 but production has not been significant so far.

King County has one of the few courthouses still enclosed by a fence. The county is building a new administration building next door to the old courthouse in Guthrie but the old building will be preserved. It was built in 1914.

KING COUNTY

This is another county named for a man from Gonzales. William P. King marched to San Antonio with 31 of his neighbors in February of 1836 to reinforce William B. Travis' doomed garrison at the Alamo. King was 24 years old when the Mexicans killed him and the other members of the "Immortal 32" and the rest of the Alamo defenders on March 6th.

King County was created by the legislature in 1876. There were only a few cowmen here at the time. The population grew to 40 by 1880 and there were almost 200 people here by the time the county government was organized in 1891. Two tiny settlements named Ashville and Guthrie contended for the honor and commercial advantage of becoming the county seat. Ashville lost and disappeared. Guthrie became the commercial center and principal town in the county. But it hasn't grown much. The population of the county is under 500 and fewer than 200 people live in Guthrie.

The most conspicuous landmark in Guthrie is the headquarters house of the 6666 Ranch on the western edge of town. This ranch surrounds the town and spreads along both sides of U.S. Highway 83 for miles to the north and south of Guthrie. The 6666 was founded by the late Samuel Burk Burnett. He started ranching in Denton County and then moved to Wichita County in the 1870s. He bought the Eight Ranch here in King County in 1900 and put his 6666 brand on it. The spread here has been the main base of the Burnett Ranches since about 1910.

Samuel Burnett was brought to Texas from Missouri by his parents when he was six. The Burnetts settled in Denton County in 1856. Samuel started driving cattle to Kansas for his father and his neighbors when he was 16. He started working for himself in 1870 when he bought his first herd of cattle. The story that Burnett won his ranch when he drew four sixes in a poker game has been circulated around Texas for years.

1

1) *The fences of the 6666 Ranch line U.S. 83 on both sides for miles north and south of Guthrie.*
2) *Latham Withers' costume would not impress an urban cowboy. But Lath can do things urban cowboys have only heard about. He has been a top hand on the Four Sixes for 36 years. Philip Morris makes some of the Marlboro Country pictures on this ranch. Lath has not appeared in any of them. He doesn't smoke.*
3) *The Four Sixes Supply House is actually a general store built about 1900.*

3

But poker had nothing to do with it. Samuel Burnett bought the 6666 brand with that first herd he bought. And he bought all the ranches he owned.

Burnett was one of the first ranchers to start improving the native Texas beef cattle and he was one of the organizers of the Texas Cattle Raisers' Association. Luck did not make him a rancher but his choice of ranch lands proved lucky for his heirs. Burnett ranches produce great quantities of oil and gas.

Burnett built the big ranch headquarters house at Guthrie in 1917. But he was living most of the time by then in Fort Worth and doing his traveling in a splendid private railway car he called the 6666 Special. Burnett died in 1922 at the age

Home on the range. The headquarters house on the 6666 Ranch built by the late Samuel Burk Burnett. The ranch is usually spoken of as the Four Sixes. Cowboys call it The Sixes.

of 73. The ranches are still owned by his heirs. Ranch manager J. J. Gibson and his family live in the big house at Guthrie now.

The oil in this county was discovered in 1943. There is a little farming here, but ranching still is much the bigger factor in the economy.

KNOX COUNTY

The legislature created this county first in 1858. The area was on the frontier at the time and everybody thought the frontier was moving westward. But the frontier forts were abandoned and the Indians got bolder and the frontier moved back eastward when the Civil War started in 1861. Nobody settled here. The Indians were driven into the Oklahoma Territory by 1875. The legislature re-created this county in 1876 and a few people began to drift in. The name is the same one the legislature chose in 1858. It honors the memory of President Washington's first secretary of war. He was General Henry Knox.

Robert D. Goree played a major role in settling Knox County. Goree came here as a rancher in 1882. He got interested in agriculture and began encouraging immigrants to come in and take up farming. Some Norwegians came in and settled Gilliland in the 1890s. German Catholics came in and settled Rhineland in 1895.

Benjamin was the first town in the county. Hilory Bedford started it in 1884 when he subdivided some land he owned near the center of the county. Bedford named the town for his

1

2

1) *The Knox County Courthouse in Benjamin is one of those the WPA built in 1935 in the standard WPA style.*
2) *The jail is included in the present courthouse so the county no longer needs the old stone jail built in 1887. It is now a private residence.*
3) *The population of Benjamin has been declining and many of the businesses have left. A bank was on this corner lot opposite the courthouse. It closed years ago. The building was torn down but for some reason the demolishers left the vault standing. There is no bank in Benjamin now.*
4) *This is the original school house built in Benjamin in 1896. It is now a lodge hall and community meeting place.*

3

4

son and the first settlers imported enough lumber from Wichita Falls to build 12 houses the first year. Benjamin was chosen to be the county seat when the county government was organized in 1886. It is still the county seat, but Benjamin has not grown much. The population is less than 300. Munday, Knox City and Goree all are bigger but they are not big, either. The population of the county is just over 5,000. This is about half what it was when the trend to fewer and bigger farms started in the 1940s. The Wichita Valley Railroad built its line from Wichita Falls to Stamford in the early 1900s. The line came through Munday in southeast Knox County because the people of Munday had the foresight to put up some

1) The Brazos and the South Wichita cross Knox County. U.S. Highway 82 runs along the divide between the two watersheds east of Benjamin. Rain falling on the north side of the highway drains into the South Wichita and eventually into the Mississippi. Water falling on the south side of the highway drains into the Brazos. There is some rugged scenery in both directions.

2) The little village of Rhineland is dignified by St. Joseph's Catholic Church. German Catholics established the parish in 1895. This church was built in 1930.

2

money to make sure it did. The line missed the little hamlet of Goree so the residents of Goree moved their hamlet a couple of miles to get on the tracks. They found out then that the deal Munday had made with the railroad provided that Munday would be the only place in the county the trains would stop.

The Handbook of Texas says the people of Goree used to put soap on the rails to force the trains to stop when somebody from Goree wanted to get on board. But the same source says the railroad did not begin stopping regularly at Goree until the people of Goree reimbursed Munday for part of the bonus Munday had paid the railroad. Goree was named for the early settler Robert D. Goree.

The Brazos River runs through Knox County. There are several big irrigated farms and substantial cotton and grain crops are grown mostly in the southern part of the county. Farming is more important than ranching in this county's economy. There is some oil and gas but Knox County does not rank high on the list of oil and gas producers in Texas. The oil was discovered in 1946.

This part of Foard County was once part of Hardeman County. There was a town here in the 1880s. It was called Margaret and it was the county seat of Hardeman County. Little remains of Margaret except a state marker and this old house.

FOARD COUNTY

This county was created by the legislature in 1891 from parts of four of the counties created in 1876. A rancher named J. G. Witherspoon petitioned the legislature to take some land away from Hardeman, Knox, King and Cottle counties to form a new county. The effort succeeded because a lot of other landowners joined in the petition and because somebody had the good judgment to propose naming the proposed new county for Confederate veteran Robert Foard. *The Handbook of Texas* observes that Major Foard at the time was a law partner of the main man on the senate committee that handled the petition.

The original county seat of Hardeman County is now in Foard County. Margaret was established about 1884 and named for Margaret Wesley. She was said to have been the first white child born in Hardeman County. The Hardeman County government moved to Quanah before this area was detached from that county and made part of Foard County. Margaret has all but disappeared. Crowell is the county seat and principal town of Foard County.

Farming and ranching are the chief enterprises here. There is a little oil and gas production, too. The oil was discovered in 1929.

The most important historic site here is on the south bank of the Pease River near the mouth of Mule Creek at the northern edge of the county. Cynthia Ann Parker was recaptured from the Comanches at this site. The Indians had kidnapped Cynthia Ann from her family's home in Limestone County in 1836 when she was nine years old. Ranger Captain Lawrence "Sul" Ross didn't know Cynthia Ann was here

1

2

1) Texas Rangers recaptured Cynthia Ann Parker from the Comanches here on the bank of the Pease River in what is now northern Foard County. Cynthia Ann had been a captive for 24 years and she had married a Comanche chief.
2) Crowell has been the county seat since Foard County was organized in 1891. The town was named for landowner George T. Crowell. The present courthouse was built in 1910.
3) An old firehouse at 116 North Main in Crowell has been turned into a museum. This building and the courthouse survived but most of the buildings in Crowell were damaged by a tornado in 1942. The museum is open Mondays through Saturdays and on Sunday afternoons. There is no fee for admission.

3

when he and about 60 rangers and volunteers swooped down upon the Comanche camp on the river bank on a windy December day in 1860. Ross was just bent upon punishing any Comanches he could find for a raid Comanches had made a couple of months earlier in Parker County. The tribe camped here that day was one headed by Chief Peta Nocona. Cynthia Ann was married to the chief. They had three children. *The Handbook of Texas* says the Ross party killed Nocona in the encounter on the Pease. Other accounts say the chief and his son Quanah and the other braves were all away from the camp at the time. T. R. Fehrenbach says in *Lone Star* that there were only women and children and a few Mexican slaves in the camp when Ross attacked.

All the authorities agree that Ross and his party recognized

This is called the Foard County Museum but it actually is private property. This is the headquarters house on the old McAdams Ranch, at the end of Farm Road 654 about 15 miles west of Crowell. It has been preserved as an example of how an early Plains ranch family lived. Open by appointment. Phone 817-474-2360.

that one of the women they found in the camp was not an Indian. They took her back to their camp in Throckmorton County and Issac Parker came out from his home in Tarrant County and verified that the woman was his dead brother's daughter.

The Parkers took Cynthia Ann back into their family but she never readjusted to white ways. The infant daughter she had with her when the rangers liberated her died about three years later and Cynthia Ann died shortly afterward. Her son Quanah went on to become war chief of his tribe. "Sul" Ross went on to a distinguished military and political career. He was governor of Texas from 1887 until 1891 and president of Texas A&M from 1891 to 1898.

COTTLE COUNTY

This is another county named for one of the men from Gonzales killed at the Alamo. George Washington Cottle was born in Tennessee and he lived briefly in Missouri before he came to Texas and settled in the Green C. DeWitt Colony on the Lavaca River. He was one of the "Immortal 32" volunteers the town of Gonzales sent to San Antonio to reinforce the garrison at the Alamo just before it fell to the Mexicans on March 6, 1836.

Cottle County was created by the legislature in 1876 when Texans were beginning to feel that the Comanche menace in this part of the world had been eliminated. Several big ranches were grazing cattle on the open range here by the 1880s. A few settlers had moved in by the 1890s and there was some farming by 1900. More land is devoted to ranching than to farming still, but the cotton and grain crops earn most of the income here. There are several thousand acres under irrigation. Oil was discovered in Cottle County in 1955 but pro-

1

2

3

1) *A bust of former State Representative Bill Heatley has a place of honor outside the Cottle County Courthouse in Paducah. Heatley has a law office across the street. The Courthouse was built in 1930. There is a small museum in the county library in the basement.*

2) *The oldest house in Paducah is this place at 1314 Easley Street. It was built in 1896 by Joe Gober. He was the first sheriff here. The asbestos shingles don't add much, but they help keep the wind out.*

3) *Carl Darr can pick pecans off the trees in his backyard in Paducah with the bullwhips he makes. Carl is 84. He started making custom saddles and bullwhips in Paducah after he retired from his job as a cowboy on the Four Sixes Ranch in 1944.*

duction is not significant.

The county government was organized in 1892 and rancher J. J. McAdams offered part of his ranch in the middle of the county as a site for the county seat. The voters approved the offer. Residents of the rival town of Cattle claimed it was because people were offered free lots if they voted for the McAdams site. But the losers always said things like that after a county seat election. Cattle disappeared. The new town on the McAdams site was named Paducah because two of the new county officials came from the Kentucky town of the same name. Paducah has been the county seat ever since.

The population of this county reached a high of 7,000 in the 1940s when people still thought they could subsist on family farms. It has been declining ever since and stands now around 3,000.

The town of Swearingen is the former headquarters of the OX Ranch and the town was named for one of the ranch owners.

The town of Cee Vee got its unusual name because it is on land that was part of the old CV Ranch.

1   2

*1) The Motley County Courthouse built in Matador in 1891 burned in the
1940s. The present courthouse was built in 1948. Former residents return here
for the Old Settlers' Reunion on the fourth weekend in August every year.
2) The fire that destroyed the 1891 courthouse spared the county jail built the
same year. It is still in use but not often.*

MOTLEY COUNTY

The legislature meant to name this county for Dr. Junius
W. Mottley. The doctor came to Texas sometime in 1835 in
time to take part in the convention that wrote the Declaration
of Independence at Washington-on-the-Brazos on March 2,
1836. Mottley signed the declaration and then joined the
army. He was wounded at San Jacinto on April 21, and he
died on the battleground that night. He certainly had done
enough to earn the gratitude of Texans. His name was spelled
correctly on several documents. But the legislature managed
to spell it wrong in the bill creating Motley County in 1876.
The mistake never was corrected.

The history of Motley County has been dominated by one
enterprise almost from the beginning. That enterprise is the
Matador Ranch. There were only buffalo hunters here when
the county was created. There was a big buffalo hunters'
camp called Tee Pee City east of the present town of
Matador. And one of the hunters built a dugout at Ballard
Springs. Cattlemen A. M. Britton and H. H. Campbell took
over that dugout after the hunter abandoned it and they made
it the headquarters for the ranching partnership they formed
in 1878.

Britton found a financial angel a little later and turned the
enterprise into the Matador Cattle Company. Campbell was
the manager until the Motley County government was
organized in 1891. Then he was elected county judge. The
Matador was running 60,000 head of cattle on 300,000 acres
of land in Motley, Dickens, Floyd and Cottle counties by that
time, and it had been bought by a syndicate in Scotland.

35

1

2

1) The headquarters house on the Matador Ranch was built of limestone in 1917. The house is on a hill just south of the town of Matador on State Highway 70. The ranch owners arranged with the Quanah, Acme and Pacific Railroad to extend a rail line to the ranch in 1912. The line passed eight miles to the south of Matador. That was fine for the ranch but it didn't do anything for the town. So the citizens of Matador formed the Motley County Railroad Company to build a line between Matador and the Quanah, Acme and Pacific tracks at Roaring Springs. The service started in 1919 and continued until it was abandoned in 1936. No trace is left of the Motley County Railroad except a marker where the depot was.
2) Roaring Springs doesn't have rail service anymore, either. But the old depot is still in good shape. It's the oldest building in town. The city of Roaring Springs owns it.

The Scottish company expanded the ranch and collaborated with the Quanah, Acme and Pacific Railroad to extend a line into the county. The company managed to pay regular dividends until 1951 when it sold out to an American syndicate.

H. H. Campbell and the Matador Ranch founded the town of Matador. There was no town anywhere in Motley County when it came time to choose a county seat. It is said that the ranch sent a few cowboys to open temporary businesses at the town site so Matador could qualify to be designated the county seat. Those "businesses" closed the next day but others eventually opened and Matador has been the county seat since 1891.

Oil was discovered in Motley County in 1957 but there have not been any gushers. Production is at a very modest level. There are some irrigated farms and the cotton, grain and peanut crops now earn about as much as the livestock here. About 2,000 people live in the county. More than half of them are in Matador.

1) This was the headquarters house of the Shoe Bar Ranch. The ranch was the first one in Hall County and this is one of the oldest houses in the county. It is adobe, built about 1884, 10 miles west of Memphis.
2) The county museum occupies the old First National building on the square in Memphis. The museum is free and open afternoons except Sundays.

HALL COUNTY

This county had no settlers at all when the legislature created it from part of the old Bexar and Young districts in 1876. The Fort Worth and Denver Railroad laid tracks across the northeast corner of the county in 1887 and then built a branch line to Lubbock that crossed the county. The population grew fairly rapidly during those years. There were more than 20,000 people in Hall County by 1930 but many were small farmers and the drought of the thirties ruined them. The population has been declining since 1930. It is under 6,000 now.

The first settler in the county was John Fields. He came in 1877 and built a dugout near the present town of Parnell. There were 36 people living in the county in 1880 when Thomas Bugbee and L. G. Coleman started the Shoe Bar Ranch west of the present town of Memphis. Bugbee had interests in several other ranches, too. He was credited with introducing some of the feed grains now so important in the Panhandle. Bugbee also was one of the first landowners in this area to use harvesters and tractors.

Hall County had about 200 permanent residents in 1890 when the county government was organized. The residents voted to put the county seat at the town of Memphis on the new Fort Worth and Denver Railroad. The town was just getting started. The post office was established the same year.

1

2

1) The Hall County Courthouse in Memphis was built in 1923. It has had some remodeling. The tinted windows are not original.

2) This building was originally a hunting lodge on the Mill Iron Ranch. It was more verandah than anything else then. The lodge was remodeled and turned into ranch headquarters after the original headquarters house burned in 1896. The Mill Iron Ranch house sits on the bluff overlooking the Prairie Dog Town Fork of the Red River at the eastern edge of Hall County.

3) The Mill Iron house is on the outskirts of what is left of the town of Estelline. This was an important railroad junction when rail connections were more important than they are today. The Fort Worth and Denver main line comes through here and there is a branch line between Estelline and Plainview. Estelline once was the biggest shipping point on the Fort Worth and Denver.

3

Memphis apparently was named for the city in Tenneseee.

Hall County was named for one of the early Anglo adventurers. Warren D. C. Hall was born in North Carolina in 1788. He came to Texas the first time as a member of the Gutierrez-Magee Expedition. Texas was still Spanish then. Jose Bernardo Gutierrez was one of the Mexicans trying to end the Spanish rule. U.S. authorities carefully looked the other way while he recruited an expedition in the United States. Augustus William Magee was one of the Americans he recruited. Magee was a former U.S. Army officer. Several hundred other Americans joined the expedition. They invaded Texas in 1812. Magee died after the expedition cap-

1

1) One of the great early western music stars grew up in Hall County. The late Bob Wills was born in 1905 in Groesbeck. But his family moved to a farm near Turkey while Bob was still a boy.

2) This monument in Turkey recalls that Bob worked as a barber in the daytime and played country dances at night until he went to Fort Worth and organized his first band. Bob led the Lightcrust Doughboys and the Texas Playboys. He wrote **San Antonio Rose** and many other popular tunes.

2

tured Goliad. But the invaders went on to capture San Antonio before the dissension that eventually wrecked the expedition broke out.

Warren Hall and about 100 other Americans quit and returned to the United States in disgust because Gutierrez was condoning the execution of captured Spanish officers. Other differences caused Gutierrez to quit and leave San Antonio himself just before the Spanish got organized and put an end to the invasion.

Hall was in Texas again briefly in 1817 helping the French privateer Louis-Michel Aury seize Galveston in the name of the Mexican rebels. He came back again in 1835 to join the Texas revolution against Mexico. He served brief terms as adjutant general of the Texas Army and secretary of war for the republic. Hall died in Galveston in 1867, nine years before the legislature named this county for him.

No significant oil or gas deposits have been found in Hall County. Much of the land is in ranches, still, but farming earns far more money. Cotton and grains are the principal crops.

1

1) *Downtown Childress looked like this in 1902. The windmill stood in the middle of the intersection of Main Street and Avenue C for nearly 20 years. It was the original city water system. Old settlers come back here for a reunion every year in July.*

2) *The original Childress County Courthouse in Childress was destroyed by fire in October of 1891. The same year the county built this new courthouse. If it were standing today it would be protected by law. But there was no law protecting old courthouses in the 1930s when the county commissioners here decided to tear this building down. Childress County is the smallest county in the Panhandle. It was named for the author of the Texas Declaration of Independence.*

2

CHILDRESS COUNTY

This county was created in 1876 at the same time most of the other counties in this end of the state were created. Development was slow until the Fort Worth and Denver came through on its way to Colorado. The railroad finished its line in this county in 1887. The county government was organized the same year. The towns of Henry and Childress City contested for the county seat with a result a little different from the usual. Childress City built a frame courthouse. But then there was a compromise. The courthouse was moved to Henry and the name of Henry was changed to Childress. Childress quickly became the biggest town in the county. It still is.

Childress and Childress County both were named for George Campbell Childress. It is a little surprising that the legislature did not get around to naming a county for Childress before 1876. Maybe it was because he never succeeded at anything else after he wrote the Texas Declaration of Independence.

1

2

3

1) The present Childress County Courthouse was built in 1939.

2) An old county jail building built on a corner of the courthouse square in the 1920s has been converted to a county museum. It is open weekday afternoons. There is no charge for admission.

3) One of the upstairs rooms in the county museum is furnished like a 1900's dining room, except for the AC outlet by the window. The card in the window instructs the iceman to leave 100 pounds of ice in the icebox. The iceman would expect to find the door unlocked if the householder was away. People seldom worried about locking their doors then.

George Childress was a lawyer and a newspaperman in Tennessee before he came to Texas in 1836. He was well connected. His family was friendly with President Andrew Jackson's family. He was a nephew of the Texas empresario Sterling Robertson. Childress had only been in Texas a few weeks when the Convention of 1836 convened at Washington-on-the-Brazos. But he was chosen to be a delegate. He got himself chosen chairman of the committee to write the Declaration of Independence the same way most chairmen get chosen. Childress made the motion that a committee be appointed. The motion was approved and Convention Chairman Richard Ellis made Childress chairman of the committee. Historians generally agree that Childress wrote the declaration without any help from other members of the committee and there is some evidence that he wrote it before the Convention began. It was ready to be voted on the day after the committee was named to write it, anyway.

Childress was appointed a special agent to go to Washington and try to get the United States government to

This old steam locomotive used to pull trains for the Fort Worth and Denver line. It is on display on the site where the Fort Worth and Denver depot stood, between Main and Commerce in Childress. The engine was built in 1911 and it traveled more than two million miles before it was retired.

recognize Texas as an independent republic. He didn't make any headway with that assignment and after a couple of months he returned to Tennessee. Childress came to Texas on three occasions during the days of the republic. He was trying to get a law practice going. He failed, and he killed himself in Galveston in 1841.

Oil was discovered in Childress County in 1961 but there is not much production. There is substantial ranching but farming is the biggest money-maker here and the big crops are cotton and grains. Ranching was the only enterprise here until 1886. That was the year the first farmers came in. Virtually the entire county was occupied before that by the Shoe Nail and OX ranches. About 5,000 people live in Childress now. Only about 1,000 live in all the rest of the county. The little community of Kirkland originally was in Hardeman County. The residents moved the town seven miles south and west into Childress County in 1887 to get on the new railroad.

There was a little town called Loco at the northern end of the county. It was named for the loco weed. That was a name the early ranchers gave to a plant that caused cows to act silly when they ate it. Loco has vanished. Somebody has stolen the historical marker that used to stand beside U.S. 83 near the site. And the former residents have to hold their Old Settlers' Reunions now at Waterloo in the next county.

HARDEMAN COUNTY

Hardeman County was named for two brothers from Tennessee, and the county seat was named for the last war chief of the Quahadi Comanche tribe. Bailey Hardeman and his brother Thomas came to Texas in the fall of 1835. They

1

2

3

*1) Comanche Chief Quanah Parker ter-
rorized Texans before he gave up the
hopeless fight in 1875. Then he became a
folk hero. Many Texans were proud that
he had some white blood. They thought
he couldn't have been such a classy chief
without it. The principal town in
Hardeman County is named for the chief.
2) The town of Margaret on the Pease
River was the original county seat of
Hardeman County. The government
moved to Quanah in 1890. The present
courthouse was built in 1907.
3) This old jail on Green Street in Quanah
is now a museum, open Saturday, Sunday
and Monday afternoons.*

immediately joined in the preliminaries of the revolution.
Bailey Hardeman was a delegate to the convention of 1836
where he signed the Declaration of Independence. He was
secretary of the treasury in David Burnet's interim government during the revolution. Bailey died a few months after
San Jacinto. His brother Thomas served in the Congress of
the Republic and in the state legislature before he died in
1854.

Quanah Parker was the son of Comanche Chief Peta
Nocona and the Comanche captive Cynthia Ann Parker. He
led the Quahadi Comanches in the final years of their
freedom, and he led them to the Oklahoma reservation in
1875 after Ranald Mackenzie's troops destroyed their camps
and killed all their horses.

Quanah had a talent for making the best of the inevitable.
He got along very well in the white man's world after he
learned not to blow out the flames in the gas lights. Weldon
Hart has written that Quanah almost lost his life learning that

1) A few people still live at Medicine Mounds but the town has expired. The price showing on the gas pumps is 29 cents a gallon. Medicine Mounds was named for a cluster of hills venerated by the Indians.

2) A marker south of Chillicothe celebrates some work that made possible some of what has happened on the Plains.

TEXAS AGRICULTURAL EXPERIMENT STATION, SUBSTATION NO. 12
HOME OF HYBRID SORGHUMS
FORAGE CROP FIELD STATION AT WHICH IN 1909 (WHEN SITUATED 6 MI. NE) WAS PLANTED THE UNITED STATES' FIRST SUDAN GRASS, A SORGHUM ESPECIALLY ADAPTABLE TO SEMI-ARID REGIONS. THE UNITED STATES DEPARTMENT OF AGRICULTURE HAD BROUGHT THE SEED FROM KHARTUM, AFRICA. HERE ENSUED MORE THAN A HALF-CENTURY OF SORGHUM BREEDING UNDER SUPERVISION OF A. B. CONNER, J. R. QUINBY, J. C. STEPHENS AND OTHER SCIENTISTS, CULMINATING IN HYBRID SEED FOR MORE PRODUCTIVE CROPS THAT REVOLUTIONIZED THE AGRICULTURE OF THE GREAT PLAINS. (1971)

3) The Copper Breaks State Park at the southern edge of Hardeman County is one of the state's Class I parks with the usual fees for admission and for camping. The park is on a picturesque site overlooking the Pease River. There is a small lake with a boat ramp, a nature trail, an amphitheater and a number of campsites. The park headquarters building has a small museum with Indian artifacts and some photographs of the early ranches.

4) There is some copper in the canyons along the Pease here. General George B. McClellan of the U.S. Army was one of the people misled into thinking money could be made from the copper. The general raised and lost a small fortune trying to establish a copper mine here in the early 1870s. The copper is imbedded in clay. McClellan and company never found a way to get it out.

44

Abandoned farmhouses like this stand in the vast cotton and grain fields all over the Plains. They are relics of the days when families tried to support themselves on small farms. They are left standing because they are useful for storage or because the farmers using the land are only leasing. The old shacks will all fall down soon and there will be nothing left to remind the Texans of the future that this was not always a land of plenty.

lesson in a Fort Worth hotel room. He learned a lot of other lessons, too. He made friends with Charles Goodnight and some of the other big men on the ranges he once thought of as his own. He hunted wolves with Theodore Roosevelt. Notoriety became fame.

The Fort Worth and Denver Railroad put out the word in 1886 that it would be building a line through Hardeman County. There was the usual scramble to organize towns on the route. The public's opinion of the Comanche chief had changed so much by then that Quanah was the name the promoters chose for the railroad town that was to become the county seat. Quanah Parker visited the town several times.

Hardeman County had been created originally in 1858. It was re-created in 1876 and organized in 1884. The little settlement of Margaret on the Pease River was about the only town in the county at the time and it was the county seat until 1890 when the people of Quanah promoted the election that caused the government to be moved to Quanah.

Hardeman County had a population of about 11,000 in 1940. It is about 6,000 now. Oil was discovered in the county in 1944 but production is at a fairly modest rate. Much of the land is in ranches but the main business here is farming. The big crops are wheat and cotton.

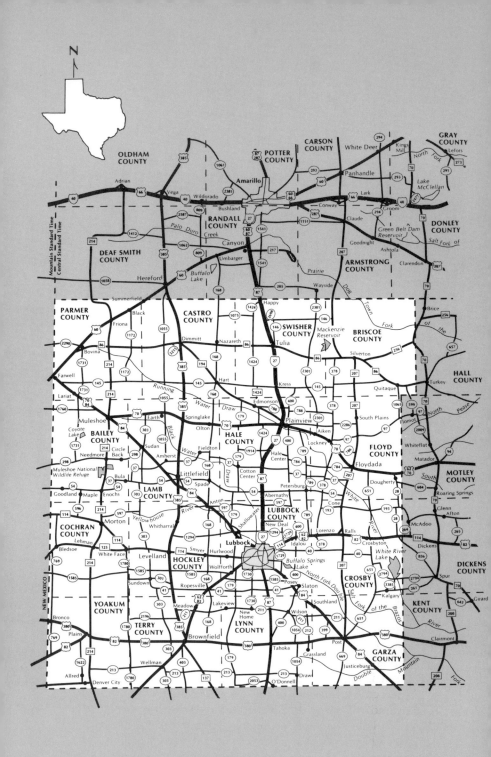

Lubbock and the High Plains

Lubbock, Crosby, Garza, Lynn, Terry,
Yoakum, Cochran, Hockley, Lamb,
Bailey, Parmer, Castro, Swisher, Hale,
Floyd and Briscoe counties.

No one is certain how the High Plains came to be called the "Llano Estacado." The term is Spanish and it translates to "Staked Plain." This is a plateau west of and several hundred feet higher than the Rolling Plains. It is almost perfectly flat. Some of the early travelers compared it to a sea. They found almost no landmarks. The most likely explanation of the term "Staked Plain," then, is that the early travelers had to make their own landmarks with stakes.

The landmarks on the Plains today are grain elevators, feedmills and cotton gins. The first enterprise here, after the buffalo were killed off, was ranching. Some of the famous early ranches were here and some are still here. There was some farming by the late 1880s and some irrigation by 1910. But promoters and real estate agents were undecided for a long time whether to call attention to the possibility of irrigating with underground water. Some were afraid any emphasis on irrigation would tip possible buyers off to the fact that it does not rain much here.

Irrigated farming did increase gradually until about 1940 and rapidly after that. Some cotton was being grown on irrigated land in Lubbock County by the middle 1930s. Now about 25 percent of America's cotton is grown in 20 counties here on the High Plains. This is one of the most important agricultural areas in the world. Its hub is the city of Lubbock.

1   2

1) *Workmen building a reservoir here in the 1930s turned up some old bones. Archaeologists hailed it as a major discovery but serious exploration did not begin until about 1970. The site is called Lubbock Lake. It is in Yellowhouse Draw just outside Loop 289, just north of U.S. 84. Visitors sometimes are admitted to the site when there is digging going on but this happens only for short periods during the summers. There are no ruins here, only bones and crude tools but some experts believe they may learn from the artifacts at Lubbock Lake whether there were humans living in this part of the world earlier than 12,000 years ago.*

2) *A replica of a Comanche Indian camp is one of the features in the fine Museum of Texas Tech University in Lubbock. They were relative newcomers but the Comanches were the Indians in possession when Texans first came to these Plains.*

LUBBOCK COUNTY

Lubbock is one of the places in Texas where archaeologists have found the bones of extinct animals together with stone tools made by man. This evidence that humans were living here 10 thousand to 12 thousand years ago was found at the Lubbock Lake Archaeological Site in west Lubbock. The site is a National Historic Landmark. Excavation is still continuing.

The whole southern half of Lubbock County was the IOA Ranch from about 1885 until the middle 1890s. The IOA was owned by speculators in Iowa and run by hired managers. Rustlers and drought prevented the outfit from making any profit and the disappointed owners sold off the last of the land and cattle in 1896. The last manager of the ranch was Rollie Burns. He was one of the founders of the town that became the city of Lubbock.

Lubbock County was created by the legislature in 1876. There were only buffalo hunters here but a few cattlemen began to move in shortly after the county was created. The

1

2

3

1) The Museum of Texas Tech is housed in one of the several striking new buildings on the busy Tech campus. This school started as Texas Technological College in 1923. It became a university in 1969 and it now includes a law school and a medical school.

2) The Museum of Texas Tech includes a large outdoor annex known as the Ranching Heritage Center.

3) Authentic buildings and equipment and implements are displayed in a natural setting. Admission to the main museum building is free but there is a small fee for the tour of the Ranching Heritage Center.

4) The Church of Christ established Lubbock Christian College as a junior college in 1957. The first buildings were castoffs from the Air Force bases in the area. But the campus on 19th Street has a complement of permanent buildings now. Lubbock Christian has been an accredited senior college since 1972.

4

1

1) *The trend away from downtown locations to the fancy suburban shopping malls has affected Lubbock as it has almost every city in Texas. But Lubbock has done a creditable job of keeping the downtown area alive and attractive with improvements like the new convention and civic center.*

2) *The present courthouse in Lubbock was built in 1950. Lubbock boosters call their city "big friendly Lubbock." It is not just boosterism. The open hospitality and willingness to help others that once characterized most of Texas still prevails on the Plains. One of the stories told about this part of the state is that the Creator made it toward the end of a day. He left it unfinished and thought He would add the rivers and lakes and greenery the next day. But He decided when He saw it the next morning just to leave it the way it was and make some people who would like it. Anyway, some people do like it and there is much to like about these people.*

3) *His music was controversial and he was not universally popular here while he was living, but this park area is dedicated to the late rock musician Buddy Holly of Lubbock. His work influenced the Beatles and all other rock musicians, and his reputation has grown considerably since he was killed in a plane crash. Mack Davis also lived in Lubbock for a time and John Denver attended high school here.*

2

3

first settlers were George Singer and his wife. They opened a trading post where the military road between Fort Griffin and Fort Sumner crossed the road between Fort Elliott and Fort Stockton. The site was about five miles northwest of the present city of Lubbock in Yellowhouse Canyon. The Singer store became the first post office in the county.

W. E. Rayner laid out a townsite in 1890 on some land he

1) Preston Smith was born in Central Texas but his family moved to the Plains when he was a boy. Smith started in Lubbock the political career that led him to the governor's office. He was governor from 1969 to 1973. He is now in the banking business in Lubbock.
2) The Lubbock Municipal Garden-Arts Center is in a landscaped park on a small lake on University Drive. The planting here features chrysanthemums. These flowers do well in this climate and Lubbock claims to be the chrysanthemum capital.

1

2

owned south of the Yellowhouse near the present campus of Texas Tech University. Rollie Burns and F. E. Wheelock laid out a town north of the canyon a short time later. Rayner called his town Monterrey. Burns and Wheelock called their town Lubbock. Both towns offered lots for little or nothing to attract settlers. Monterrey had a population of 40 and Lubbock had 50 people when the promoters decided to merge their towns. Settlers and buildings were moved to a new location. The new town was named Lubbock and it was designated the county seat when the county government was organized in 1891. One of the buildings moved from the original settlement of Lubbock to the new town was a hotel with 18 rooms. The Singers moved their store to the new Lubbock.

Lubbock and Lubbock County were named for a hero of the Civil War. Thomas S. Lubbock was born in South Carolina. He was in New Orleans in 1835 when Texans were recruiting men there to help them fight the Mexicans. Lub-

1

2

1) The Mackenzie State Park is actually operated by the City of Lubbock. It is in a low area just east of downtown, where the Yellowhouse Draw and Blackwater Draw meet to form the Double Mountain Fork of the Brazos. The city is developing a series of lakes in this valley to create what will be one of the biggest urban parks in America.

2) The First United Methodist Church on Broadway at Avenue M in downtown Lubbock has some of the biggest stained glass windows in the world.

3) The biggest cottonseed mill in the world is owned and operated by the Plains Co-Op. Cottonseed yields a valuable oil. It is used for stock feed, too. The Plains Co-Op is now also making flour from cottonseed. Lubbock is the second biggest inland cotton market in the world.

3

1) The Lubbock County Museum has an assortment of antique farm machinery on display at Avenue G and 9th Street, in Shallowater. The museum is open daily and there is no fee for admission.

2) This old locomotive sits on the town square in Slaton. There is also a small museum in Slaton at 115 North 8th Street. It is open afternoons except Sundays and Mondays. There is no admission fee.

1

2

bock joined the New Orleans Greys and took part in the Siege of Bexar that put Texans in possession of the Alamo in December of 1835. He later went to New Mexico with Texas President Mirabeau Lamar's Santa Fe Expedition. Lubbock and most of the others were captured and imprisoned by the Mexicans, but Lubbock managed to escape. He was in business in Houston when the Civil War began. He helped B. F. Terry recruit 1,000 men for the Confederate Army. This force became the Eighth Texas Cavalry. But it was always better known as Terry's Texas Rangers. Terry was killed in Kentucky in December of 1861. Thomas Lubbock commanded the Rangers briefly until he died in 1862.

Lubbock County has been producing oil since 1941. But crops and livestock earn more than 100 million dollars a year here and this is more than 10 times what the county's oil production is worth. The city of Lubbock has a population surging toward 200,000, a major university and two colleges, a number of factories and the biggest cottonseed mill in the world.

The Army established the Lubbock Advanced Flying School here in 1941 to train pilots. The base was re-named Lubbock Army Air Field before it closed in 1945. The Air Force put the base back in business in 1949 and named it Reese Air Force Base in honor of Lieutenant A.F. Reese. He was a native of Lubbock County, killed in WWII. The Reese Air Force Base is not open to the general public except on special occasions.

CROSBY COUNTY

Most of Crosby County is on the High Plain but the southeastern part is in the picturesque Blanco Canyon of the White River. The county was created in 1876.

There were buffalo hunters here before him and a few cattlemen grazing their stock on the open range, but the first permanent settler in Crosby County was Hank Smith. He built the first real house in the county on his small ranch in Blanco Canyon north of the present town of Crosbyton. Smith built his house of native stone and lumber he hauled out here from Fort Worth in oxcarts. That was in 1877. He also dug a well and established that there was ample underground water here.

A few farmers were in the county by 1879. They were Quakers brought in by Paris Cox. He got into the colonizing business unintentionally. Cox was operating a sawmill in Indiana when a railroad land agent came along and offered to trade him some land in Texas for the mill. The state was giving railroads great tracts of land to induce them to build new lines and the railroads could do anything they wanted to with the grants. Cox came to Texas to look at the land the railroad man was offering. He liked it. He swapped his sawmill in 1876 for 50,000 acres in northwest Crosby County.

1

1) *There was a town here once and the town that was here was the original county seat of Crosby County. What is left of Estacado is on Farm Road 1527 on the western edge of Crosby County. The Quaker settlers here were the first farmers on the Texas Plains. They called their settlement Marietta when they first established it in 1879. They changed the name to Estacado when the town was designated the county seat in 1886. The government moved away to a new town called Emma in 1890 and Estacado began to die. Emma died when the government moved from there to Crosbyton in 1911.*

2) *The man Crosby County was named for never laid eyes on it. The legislature named the county for Stephen Crosby because he was chief clerk in the state land office for a long time.*

2

Cox traveled around the northeastern states offering to sell land at 25 cents an acre to Quaker families willing to move to Crosby County. He signed up 30 families and they all headed for Texas by wagon train in 1879. The trip was more than the Quakers had bargained for. Most of them dropped out of the caravan along the way. Only seven families actually reached Crosby County. The winter of 1879 was so severe that everybody except the Cox family abandoned the little settlement in the spring of 1880.

Cox hung on and raised some crops during 1880. This helped him induce more Quakers to join him in 1881 in the settlement he was calling Marietta. He named it for Mrs. Cox. The Quakers had several good years at Marietta. The weather was benign. The crops were adequate. Everybody was encouraged by the results of this first attempt at farming on the

1) *The building on the dominant site in Crosbyton is not the courthouse. A replica of a pioneer rock house sits on the central square here. It is a replica of the house the county's first settler built on his ranch north of the present town in 1877. This is the Crosby County Pioneer Memorial Museum, open daily except Mondays during the summer, and free.*

2) *The Crosby County Courthouse sits on a corner opposite the museum. It was built in 1914.*

3) *There is an unusually pretty roadside park where U.S. 82 crosses the White River east of Crosbyton. It has a little waterfall and a hiking trail.*

High Plain. The Quaker colony was designated the county seat when the Crosby County government was organized in 1886. The name of the settlement was changed then to Estacado.

A couple of Estacado merchants bought some land a few miles south of Estacado in 1891 and promoted a new town. H. E. Hume and R. L. Stringfellow named their town Emma for Stringfellow's girl friend. The town caught on. Hume and Stringfellow promoted an election and got the county seat and the courthouse building moved from Estacado to Emma. This and a plague of grasshoppers in 1892 and a drought in 1893 finished off Estacado. But Emma didn't last long, either. The county's voters decided in another election in 1911 to move the county seat to the new town of Crosbyton. The courthouse was torn down and most of the other buildings were moved to the new county seat.

Crosbyton was established in 1908 by the C. B. Livestock Company on land the company had bought from the Two Buckle Ranch. Crosbyton got rail service in 1910 and that helped the town win the county seat.

1

2

3

1) The old John Ralls Building in Ralls is now a museum. Ralls founded this town in 1911.

2) State Highway 207 descends from the Cap Rock into the Brazos valley south of Ralls.

3) A solar power collector on Farm Road 651 south of Crosbyton is said to be the biggest such collector in the world. Heat collected at the spot where the sun strikes this reflector generates steam to power a small turbine. The turbine generates enough electricity to power one small house on a sunny day. This experiment is manned by Dr. John Reichert and Texas Tech University.

Oil was discovered in Crosby County in 1955 but it was no bonanza. Ranching is still important, but farming produces most of the income here. The county has nearly 150,000 acres under irrigation.

The county and the county seat were named for Stephen Crosby. He was chief clerk of the Texas land office from 1845 until 1867.

GARZA COUNTY

There probably is not another county in Texas that was influenced by a single individual to the degree that this county was. The individual was Charles W. Post.

The legislature created this county in 1876 and named it for a pioneer Texas family. The ranchers moved in as the buffalo hunters finished off the last of the buffaloes. The area was open range in the early days. But ranchers were leasing and buying land by the 1880s. John B. Slaughter was one of the early operators here. The Curry Comb Ranch owned most of the northwest quarter of the county for a time. There were 36 people in Garza County in 1880. A drought in 1886 forced

1) The city of Post is the county seat of Garza County. There is a statue of cereal man C.W. Post in front of the courthouse because Post founded the town and owned everything around it at one time. The courthouse was built in 1925. The statue was donated by Post's daughter Marjorie Merriweather Post.

2) C. W. Post had this home built for himself on West Main Street. The street must be one of the widest residential streets in America. The home is not ostentatious but it was built with the finest materials and fixtures and some of the interior walls were covered with leather. It is now a funeral home.

most of those people to leave. It also encouraged the survivors to begin digging wells. They found water and there was a little farming in the area by 1900. But most of the land was owned by a few big ranchers when Charles Post came on the scene in 1906.

Post was born in Illinois in 1854. He had his own business there before he was 30. He also had trouble with his stomach and his nerves. He thought overwork caused his problems and he moved to Texas to get away from the stress. Post settled in Fort Worth but he did not change his style. He soon had a ranch and a woolen mill and a real estate business. And he was having problems with his health again by 1890. He went to Michigan to be treated at the Battle Creek Sanitarium. He also saw a Christian Science practitioner. His health improved and he started his own sanitarium in Battle Creek. There he began the experiments in nutrition that produced Postum and Post Toasties and Post Bran.

Post became an important business figure and president of the National Association of Manufacturers. He opposed labor unions but he was generous with his own employees. He was convinced of the virtues of private enterprise and he believed the way to build a better world was to help more people get a stake in it. He had the money to put his ideas into practice. His cereals had made him millions. Post started

1

2

1) C. W. Post was obsessed with health most of his life because his own health was never very good. He saw to it that his town had the very best in health care. The Sanitarium he built at 117 North Avenue N in Post was the first real hospital in this part of Texas. The building is listed in **The National Register of Historic Places.** It was built in 1912 and it is now a museum, open Wednesdays.
2) The old Algarita Hotel in Post is also in **The National Register of Historic Places.** The Algarita is on Main Street, but it is no longer a hotel.
3) Burlington now operates the cotton textile mill C. W. Post founded in 1912. This was the first mill in this part of the world to take raw cotton all the way to finished textiles.

3

building homes and selling them to his workers on easy terms. He thought of Texas when he felt he needed a bigger arena.

The cereal tycoon came to Garza County and bought the Curry Comb Ranch. He divided the ranch into farms of 160 acres each. He built a house on each farm and offered the farms for sale on long terms. He laid out a town to serve as the market place for his colony. He called it Post City. Post built the business block and the hotel and a sanitarium. The town was run in the beginning by the directors of Post's Double U Company. Post City was designated the county seat when Garza County was organized in 1907. The name was changed then to Post. Charles Post encouraged his people to grow cotton. He built a gin and then built a textile mill to make sure there was a market for the cotton.

Post provided his community with everything except an abundance of rain and he tried to provide that. He spent more than 50,000 dollars trying to shake rain out of the skies with dynamite here between 1911 and 1914. He believed he caused a few showers but most people doubt it. Post was plagued with poor health all the days of his life. He had an operation

1

1) The one thing his community needed that C. W. Post could not supply was rain. But he tried mightily. Post and his crews set off hundreds of pounds of dynamite on the edge of the Cap Rock above the town in the early 1900s. There was some rain occasionally but it never was certain whether Post's experiments caused any of it. He thought they did. This roadside park is near where some of the explosions were set off. It is on U.S. 84, three miles west of Post.

2) Post's Double U Ranch on the western outskirts of Post is still owned by the Post estate.

3) Post is situated over a rich oil field. This rare sextuple well is on the west side of the city. It is one well with six pumps bringing up oil from six different levels.

2   3

for appendicitis in California in 1914 and killed himself shortly afterward. He was just 60 years old.

Only the western part of Garza County is on the High Plain. The city of Post and most of the county lie on the lower Rolling Plain. Much of the land in the county still is devoted to ranching, but farming earns more money. Oil was discovered at Justiceburg in 1926 and there is very substantial production. The oil and gas income is about three times the agricultural income here.

1

1) Tahoka has been the county seat of Lynn County since the county was organized in 1903. The town was named for a lake named by the Indians. The present courthouse in Tahoka was built in 1916. The area is noted for a lavender wildflower called the Tahoka Daisy.

2) This old windmill stands at the entrance to the Tahoka Pioneer Museum on Lockwood at Avenue J in downtown Tahoka. Enthusiasm for high school football is generally higher on the Plains than in any other part of the state. Towns identify with the high school team. The players here are called the Bulldogs and a big sign on the town water tower proclaims that Tahoka is Bulldog Country.

2

LYNN COUNTY

There is some surface water in natural depressions in this county. The Comanches and the Kiowas camped regularly at Tahoka Lake in the center of what is now Lynn County. Ranald Mackenzie's troops camped in the same area later while they were making war on the Indians. The lake was a regular stop for wagon trains and pioneer rancher C. C. Slaughter had one of his early cattle camps on the shore of Tahoka Lake. Tahoka is said to mean "deep water" or "clear water" in one of the Indian dialects.

A company of U.S. troops led by Nicholas Nolan came here in 1877 in pursuit of a Comanche raiding party. Nolan's outfit set up a base at Double Lakes and followed the Indians' trail off to the north for several days. The trail played out and the soldiers' water did, too. The troops were without water for 86 hours. Most of them made it back to Double Lakes but four of Nolan's men and all of his horses died of thirst on that march back.

Underground water makes this one of the richer agricultural areas on the Plains today. There is a little oil and some ranching. But cotton, wheat and sorghums are the big money makers in Lynn County.

The county was created by the legislature in 1876. It was

1

2

1) The T-Bar Ranch was established in Lynn County by C. O. Edwards in 1882. The headquarters house is not that old and it has had some remodeling. Much of the land is now in cotton. The T-Bar is on a local dirt road about five miles north of Tahoka.
2) The old Wilson Mercantile Company in Wilson is almost a museum. William Green founded the town and named it Wilson because he had bought the land from the Wilson County School District. Wilson flourished for a time after Green persuaded the Panhandle and Santa Fe to build a rail line through, in 1911. His son's wife has restored the brick store building Wilson put up here in 1917. It is filled with furnishings and merchandise such as it might have had in it when the town was young. This old wagon is securely chained down outside the building.

named for one of the men killed in the defense of the Alamo on March 6, 1836. Not much is known about some of the men killed at the Alamo. It is not certain whether the man this county was named for was W. Lynn or W. Linn. But the legislature decided to spell the name Lynn.

There was no rush to settle the county when it was created. The first census in 1880 showed a population of nine. C. O. Edwards established his T-Bar Ranch in the county in 1882. Four other ranches were operating in the county by 1900 and the population was up to 17. There were not many more people here when the county government was organized in 1903. The settlement of Tahoka near the lake was designated the county seat. There are about 9,000 people in Lynn County today and about a third of them live in Tahoka.

The late television star Dan Blocker grew up in the little farming community of O'Donnell on the southern edge of Lynn County. Blocker was born in Bowie County in East Texas in 1928. His parents brought him here when he was six. His father ran a store in O'Donnell and Dan went to school in O'Donnell and at Texas Military Institute in San Antonio. He started college at Hardin-Simmons in Abilene and transferred to Sul Ross in Alpine in 1947. Dan was a football star at Sul

1) *The little museum in O'Donnell is filled with tools and implements and furnishings from pioneer days. The museum is in the old First National Bank Building and it is open every day. There is no fee but donations are encouraged. O'Donnell is a railroad town named for railroad man Tom O'Donnell.*

2) *This memorial in a tiny park in the center of O'Donnell is a tribute to one of the town's former star athletes. Dan Blocker was born in Bowie County and he was buried in Bowie Bounty when he died in 1972. But he grew up here and attended school here in the 1930s and 1940s.*

Ross. He served in the infantry during the war in Korea and taught school in West Texas and New Mexico before he moved to California and started the acting career that made him rich and famous.

TERRY COUNTY

This county was named for the first leader of one of the famous cavalry regiments of the Confederate Army. Benjamin Franklin Terry was born in Kentucky in 1821. His family brought him to Texas when he was ten. He married into one of Stephen F. Austin's Old Three Hundred families and became a sugar planter in Fort Bend County. The planter families were not the leading advocates of secession generally. But Terry was for it. He went to Austin as a delegate to the 1861 convention that voted to take Texas out of the Union. He immediately went to Virginia and fought with Confederate troops against the Union Army at the First Battle of Manassas. He returned to Texas after that to organize his own regiment. Terry and Thomas Lubbock signed up 1,000 volunteers in Houston in September of 1861. The unit was designated the Eighth Texas Cavalry but it was always called Terry's Texas Rangers.

The regiment fought in several major battles including Shiloh and Chickamauga before the Confederacy gave up the

1

2

1) Terry County was named for the leader of one of the famous Confederate fighting units. Colonel B. F. Terry led Terry's Texas Rangers until he was killed in battle in December of 1861.

2) Brownfield has been the county seat since Terry County was organized in 1904. The present courthouse was built in 1925.

war. But Benjamin Terry fought only one battle with his Rangers. He was killed in the first fight at Woodsonville in Kentucky in December of 1861 at the age of forty.

This county was created in 1876 at the same time the legislature was creating 53 other counties in this end of the state. Democrats had just regained control of the state government from the Republicans and carpetbaggers. It was a time for honoring the heroes of the lost cause. Many counties and towns were named for Confederate leaders and many statues were raised on courthouse lawns during the late 1870s.

The development of Terry County followed the usual Plains pattern. The cattlemen moved in behind the buffalo hunters. They grazed their herds without worrying about ownership of the real estate for the first few years. There were five or six big ranches here by the 1890s. The state always favored farmers over ranchers in granting homestead claims and in the sales of school lands so the tracts granted or sold to any individual usually were small. But a few cattle companies were able to buy big blocks of state land. Some ranchers accumulated large holdings by having agents make homestead claims. Ranchers were able to buy large tracts when the railroads put their lands on the market in 1901 and they were always ready to buy out homesteads when the homesteaders discovered it wasn't possible to make a living on small farms here. These were some of the ways the Plains cattlemen came to possess the domains they only occupied in the beginning.

There were some serious disputes over fences when barbed

1

2

3

1) The home of one of the founders of Brownfield serves as the Terry County Heritage Museum. A. M. Brownfield built this house at East Cardwell and South B. The museum is open on Wednesday and Sunday afternoons and by appointment at other times. There is a small admission fee. Founder's Day is celebrated with a pioneer reunion here each July 4th.

2) Another historic house in Brownfield is the one F. M. Daugherty built in 1904 at 1206 Tahoka Road. Daugherty was Mrs. A. M. Brownfield's father. The original wood siding here has been plastered over. The pioneers thought they were really getting ahead in the world when they could afford cut lumber for a house. The early frame houses were a big step up from the earlier dugouts. But few of them were tight enough to keep out the winter winds so a lot of the old ones have been covered with asbestos shingles or stucco. People on the High Plains often say there is nothing between them and the North Pole except a barbed wire fence. It is a boast as much as it is a lament.

3) There are free campsites for travelers in Coleman Park off U.S. 385 in Brownfield.

4) Little is left of the earliest Terry County settlement except a small cemetery surrounded by cottonfields. The Gomez Cemetery is just off U.S. 82 west of Brownfield.

4

wire first reached the Plains. Some of the rows were between farmers and ranchers but some were between the big ranchers and the free spirits accustomed to using the open range

Texas has towns named for many famous foreign capitals. The town named for the capital of Japan is in western Terry County. Tokio has a service station, a couple of houses and a post office, Zip Code 79376.

without hindrance. The big ranch owners actually were among the first to start stringing wire fences.

The oldest settlement in Terry County is Gomez but Brownfield won the county seat when the county was organized in 1904. Brownfield was founded in 1903 and named for pioneer ranchers A. M. and M. V. Brownfield. The Santa Fe extended a branch line to Brownfield in 1917 and it is the only incorporated town in the county today.

Some ranchers despised farmers once. But the big mechanized farms earn 90 percent of the agricultural income in this county today. And the farmers and ranchers and uncounted previous landowners all benefit from the oil. Pumps in the cotton fields and on the ranges produce in an average year about twice as much revenue in Terry County as all the crops and livestock together.

YOAKUM COUNTY

This border county has some of the richest oil fields in the state. The oil was discovered in 1936 in the southern end of the county. The oil workers started a town in 1939 and called it Denver City. The new town had a population of 5,000 by 1940. The town and the oil business have had some ups and downs since then but Denver City still is the biggest town in the county and headquarters for most of the businesses related to oil.

The legislature created Yoakum County in 1876. Several cattlemen were established on the open range here by 1880. But the census of 1900 showed a total population of 26 for the county. More settlers came in during the early 1900s and there were enough people here to organize a county government by 1907. The town of Plains was designated the county seat.

Plains grew up around a dugout home built in the late 1890s by a family named Miller. The Millers claimed the land as a homestead grant. This practice was nearing its end at the time. The Republic of Texas allowed settlers to claim 320

1) Yoakum County was named for Henderson Yoakum. He was a soldier, lawyer and historian.
2) Early settlers here built little houses like this to nail down their claims to the land. This house has been preserved as a museum, at 1109 Avenue H, in Plains. It is open by appointment, 806-456-3212.

acres of public land if they lived on it and made certain improvements. The law was changed several times after Texas joined the United States. The final version of the law limited the grants to 160 acres. The grants ended in 1898 when there was no more unclaimed land. The republic and the state had granted almost five million acres of land to homesteaders by that time. But the state gave more than seven times that much land to the railroads to induce them to build the early rail lines. No railroad ever reached Plains.

The inspiration for the name of the county seat clearly was the location on the Plains. The county was named by the legislature for Henderson Yoakum. He wrote a history of Texas and one of the historical markers here observes that he was the only writer ever to have a Texas county named for him. He did some writing, but Henderson Yoakum's main business was the practice of law and he certainly was not the only lawyer to have a county named for him.

Yoakum was born in Tennessee and educated at the U.S. Military Academy. He practiced law and served in the Tennessee militia before he came to Texas in 1845. Yoakum settled his family at Huntsville. He became friendly with Sam Houston and represented Houston in several legal matters. He served with Jack Hays' Texas Rangers in the war with Mexico. Yoakum published his *History of Texas from its First Settlement in 1685 to its Annexation to the United States in 1846* in two volumes in 1855. People supposed that he got a lot of his information from Sam Houston.

Yoakum County has a number of prosperous irrigated

1   2

1) Plains has been the county seat since Yoakum County was organized. The present courthouse was built in 1949.

2) An earlier courthouse next door is still in use, too. This one was built in 1927. There is plenty of room for picnicking in the pleasant Yoakum County Park in a wooded dell at the northwest edge of Plains.

farms raising cotton and grains and there is substantial ranching here. But petroleum is overwhelmingly the biggest factor in the economy. The income from oil and gas runs around 30 times the income from agriculture.

COCHRAN COUNTY

There is a rodeo here on the second weekend in August every year. It is called the Last Frontier Rodeo. There is more than poetry in the name. Cochran County was the last county here to have enough people to organize a county government. The legislature created this border county in 1876. The Indian problem was about under control by then. But few people were attracted here because there were plenty of places easier to get to. Cochran County was remote and it was not on the way to anywhere. It still is not. The first railroad did not reach the county until many years later and it was a dead-end branch line from Lubbock. No U.S. highway crosses any part of the county yet. There are only state highways and farm and ranch roads here but they are excellent and never crowded.

Cochran County had a few cattlemen and cowboys by 1900. The census taker that year counted 25. There were 75 people in the county in 1910 including a few farmers. Some of them did not stay. The 1920 census showed the population had declined to 67. Interest in the area picked up a little after that. There was some prospecting for oil and the county government was organized in 1924. The little community of Morton in the northeast corner of the county was designated the county seat. No oil was found until 1936 and the popula-

1

2

1) Cochran County was not organized until 1924. The city of Morton has been the county seat since the beginning. The present courthouse was built in 1926. It was enlarged and remodeled in 1967.

2) The county museum in Morton lost its main building and most of its exhibits in a fire in 1980. A windmill and a couple of old wagons are still on the site at 206 Southwest 1st Street.

3) The headquarters complex for the C. C. Slaughter Ranch was built in 1917 off State Highway 214 south of Morton. There are several adobe buildings clustered around a central court in the hacienda style. Slaughter's heirs still own 16,000 acres here.

3

tion of the county and the county seat grew very slowly before that time. There are just 5,000 people in the county now. Half of them live in Morton.

The other towns in this county developed when the Santa Fe extended its branch line out here from Lubbock in 1925. The towns are Bledsoe, Lehman and Whiteface. They are all on the rail line. Bledsoe was named for the line's president. Lehman was named for the general manager. Whiteface was named for the white-faced Herefords the line's freight trains were hauling to market.

Ranching still is important here. Farming is more important and petroleum is the most important. Income from the oil and gas production is about three times what the crops and livestock earn each year.

Cochran County is another county named for a hero of the Alamo. Robert Cochran was born in Massachusetts. He lived in New Orleans briefly before he moved to Texas in 1835. Cochran joined the Texas Army in San Antonio in February of 1836. He was a private in the garrison at the Alamo when the Mexicans stormed the place on March 6th and killed all the defenders.

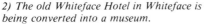

1

1) *The main unit of Girlstown, U.S.A. is on Farm Road 1780 south of Whiteface in Cochran County. Girlstown was founded by Amelia Anthony at Buffalo Gap in 1949 to care for abused, neglected and potentially delinquent girls. There are branches of Girlstown in Borger and Austin. The main dormitory here on the Whiteface campus burned in the Spring of 1981. The girls here live now in large, new cottages. They do their own cooking and housekeeping and go to school in Whiteface. Most of the girls are referred here by the juvenile courts, welfare units and school counselors.*
2) *The old Whiteface Hotel in Whiteface is being converted into a museum.*

2

HOCKLEY COUNTY

There were few natural landmarks on these plains when the first explorers came. One of the few was a yellow clay cliff bordering a draw in the northwest part of what is now Hockley County. The cliff could be seen from some distance. In certain light conditions it looked at a distance like a row of yellow buildings. The Spanish explorers called the cliff "Las Casas Amarillas." A spring in the draw at the base of the cliff made it a pleasant campground. It was frequented by explorers, Comanches, soldiers, buffalo hunters and cattlemen in turn. The name was passed down and eventually translated to "Yellow Houses." The draw came to be called Yellowhouse Draw and Yellowhouse Canyon.

A cowman named Jim Newman probably was the first to start running cattle in Yellowhouse Canyon about 1882. But he did not own the land and he moved on when the state gave title to the property to the Capitol Syndicate in 1885. It was part of the three million acres the state conveyed to the syndicate in return for building the state capitol. The syndicate's XIT Ranch had its southern division headquarters in the

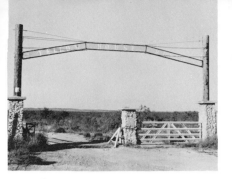

1

2

1) This part of Hockley County has been a ranch since the Indians left. This was the Yellowhouse Division of the XIT Ranch until George Littlefield bought it in 1901. It has been the Yellowhouse Ranch since then and it is still owned by the family of Littlefield's partner.

2) The Yellowhouse headquarters house looks across Yellowhouse Canyon at the scalloped canyon wall that looked like yellow houses to the early Spanish explorers. This house is not old. The original headquarters house burned several years ago.

3) I. L. Ellwood made a fortune in barbed wire and he spent part of it for land in Texas. His Spade Ranch once spread over 265,000 acres.

4) The Spade headquarters house still stands east of Levelland, off State Highway 114. Ellwood's heirs still own the ranch.

3

4

Yellowhouse until George Littlefield bought out the Yellowhouse Division in 1901.

The Yellowhouse Division occupied the northwestern quarter of the county. A big part of eastern Hockley County at the time was included in the vast Spade Ranch the Ellwood family of Illinois bought with the money from their barbed wire. The Oxsheer Ranch occupied the central and southern part of the county. The C. C. Slaughter Ranch and the Mallet Ranch had the southwestern part. There were a few

The difference between a wagon and a chuck wagon is a chuck box. Hang one on the back of a wagon and it is a chuck wagon. Charles Goodnight is credited with inventing this convenience. This one is one of the exhibits in the South Plains Museum in Levelland. The museum is open afternoons except Sundays and Mondays.

homesteaders, but very few until some of the ranches were subdivided in the early 1920s.

C. W. Post bought the Oxsheer Ranch in 1906. He laid out a town he called Hockley City in the center of the county. But Post apparently was too preoccupied with his projects in Garza County to do any promotion here.

One of the earliest settlements in Hockley County was Ropesville. W. A. Blankenship and his family settled at the site in the southeast corner of the county in 1902. There were 27 families in Ropesville by 1903. The Santa Fe built a branch line across the southeast corner of the county in 1917 and Ropesville got rail service. Another Santa Fe branch line was laid out across the middle of the county through the Hockley City site. But no one was living at Hockley City in 1921 when the county government was organized. People interested in Hockley City put on a spirited campaign for the county seat anyway. Somehow they got more votes than Ropesville did. *The Handbook of Texas* says the Hockley County Commissioners had to hold their first meeting in an automobile because there was no building in Hockley City. They fixed that by building a temporary courthouse. They changed the name of the place to Levelland. It has been the county seat and principal town ever since.

Oil was discovered in Hockley County in 1937. The county is one of the bigger oil producers in the state today. It is also one of the richest agricultural counties on the Plains with 200,000 acres of farmland under irrigation.

The name of the county seat apparently was chosen because it describes the area. The county was named for George Washington Hockley. He was one of Sam Houston's close associates. Hockley was born in Pennsylvania. He was working in Washington during the time Sam Houston was there as a congressman from Tennessee. They became friends and

1

1) Levelland was called Hockley City until it became the county seat in 1921. The present courthouse in Levelland was built in 1927.
2) Part of the art collection of the late Marjorie Merriweather Post is on display in the Fine Arts Building on the campus of South Plains College in Levelland. Marjorie Post was the daughter of C. W. Post. He laid out the town that became Levelland. The South Plains College may be the only college in the country offering a course in blue grass music.

2

Hockley moved to Tennessee during the time Houston was governor there. Hockley followed Houston on to Texas in 1835. Houston was named Commander-in-Chief of the Texas Army in 1836. He made Hockley his chief of staff. Hockley commanded the Texas artillery at San Jacinto. He died in Corpus Christi in 1854.

LAMB COUNTY
Most of this county was occupied once by the XIT Ranch. The county seat is on land where the XIT's cows once grazed.

The legislature created and named the county in 1876 when it was dividing up all the Panhandle-Plains area. The county was named for Lieutenant George A. Lamb. He came to Texas from South Carolina in 1834 and settled in what is now Walker County. Lamb joined the Texas Army in March of 1836 at Montgomery, and he was killed six weeks later at the Battle of San Jacinto.

Buffalo hunters moved in as the army was clearing out the last of the Indians. Cattlemen moved in as the hunters cleared out the last of the buffalo. The first ranchers just camped on the open range. Most of the county was still public property until the legislature awarded the Capitol Syndicate three million acres in Lamb and nine other counties in the deal for

1

2

1) Lamb County was named for one of the Texans killed at San Jacinto. But George Littlefield had the most to do with development of the county. He subdivided his big ranch into farms and founded the town of Littlefield.

2) Littlefield did not become the county seat of Lamb County until 1946. The present courthouse was built in 1953. This is Waylon Jennings' home town.

3) The American Cotton Growers' big textile mill on the outskirts of Littlefield turns out denim for Levi Strauss.

3

the state capitol building. That was in 1882. The southeast section of Lamb County became part of the Yellowhouse Division of the syndicate's XIT Ranch. Cattleman George W. Littlefield bought the entire Yellowhouse Division from the XIT in 1901. He paid two dollars an acre for about 300,000 acres.

Littlefield was born in Mississippi. His parents brought him to Texas when he was eight years old. He fought with Terry's Texas Rangers in the Civil War, and he started driving cattle from Gonzales to Kansas in 1871. Littlefield caught the cattle boom on the rise. He started grazing herds on the public lands in West Texas and New Mexico and then leased and bought ranges as that became necessary. He was rich enough by 1883 to move to Austin and start a bank. But he retained an active interest in West Texas and ranching until he died in 1920.

Littlefield operated the Yellowhouse as a ranch until about 1912. Then he made a deal with the Santa Fe Railroad to extend a rail line from Lubbock through his ranch to the New

1

2

1) The city of Littlefield provides free overnight campsites in the city park on U.S. 385 between U.S. 84 and Business 84.
2) The Sudan Hotel was a gathering place for farmers and ranchers when it was new in the early 1900s. The building has a state historical marker but it is padlocked and vacant.

Mexico border. He laid out a town on the rail line and formed the Littlefield Lands Company to sell off part of the ranch as town lots and farms. Littlefield's town became the town of Littlefield. His company drilled some wells to demonstrate the availability of water for irrigation and some of the ranch land Littlefield had bought for two dollars an acre sold as irrigated farm land for 50 and 75 dollars an acre.

There were 1,000 people living in Littlefield and on farms surrounding the town by 1917. Many of the small farmers were wiped out by a drought in 1918 and 1919. But some hung on and more moved in after the drought ended. It took about two generations for people to become really convinced that this part of the world is no place for small farmers. Today's big farmers often complain that they are going broke. But they are doing it with the advice of CPAs and with a lot more style than the farmers of the 20s and 30s did.

Lamb County still has a number of ranches. But the cotton and grain crops from the big farms earn about twice as much money as all the livestock in an average year. Almost 400,000 acres are under irrigation here.

One of the first settlements in Lamb County was Olton in the northeast part of the county. Three families settled in 1900 on some land the ranchers were not using. Their settlement became a town and it became the county seat when the county government was organized in 1908. Olton was the only settlement of any consequence then. The people of Littlefield promoted an election in 1929 to get the county seat moved to

1) Lamb County has the tallest and shortest windmills on the Plains. The tall one is a replica of a mill that stood in Yellowhouse Canyon from 1887 until it blew down in 1926. The original was 132 feet tall. The replica in Littlefield is not quite that tall.
2) The short one is a demonstration model of the mill Doug Parish's late father developed at Earth when the cost of energy caused new interest in wind power.

1

their town. They failed and they failed again in 1932 and again in 1937. But they kept trying. Littlefield won the county seat in 1946.

BAILEY COUNTY

This county on the New Mexico border was also created by the legislature in 1876 and part of it was included in the original XIT Ranch. Most of the land here was occupied by large ranches until the early 1900s. Some subdividing began about 1907. The first settlement in the county was about three miles northwest of the present town of Muleshoe. The settlement was named Hurley for the New Mexico political leader Patrick J. Hurley. Hurley had a post office and a church and a school by 1910. Real estate promoters laid out another town site near the center of the county in 1908. They called this town Virginia City and they put out a lot of ballyhoo about the crops that might be grown in the area. A few people bought land and moved to Virginia City. The drought of 1909 wiped them out, and Virginia City vanished. One writer says the cowboys joked that Virginia City's only crop was suckers.

The Santa Fe Railroad line George Littlefield engineered came through Bailey County in 1913. It missed Hurley. A new town was laid out on the rail line. It was named Muleshoe and the people at Hurley soon moved to the new town. Muleshoe

1

1) The town of Muleshoe took its name from a ranch. The town has been the county seat since the Bailey County government was organized in 1917. The present courthouse was built in 1925.

2) People from as far away as Russia contributed money for the mule memorial in Muleshoe. Texas once had more mules than any other state.

2

was designated the county seat when the county government was organized in 1917.

There is a monument to the mule at Muleshoe. This area never had any uncommon number of mules or any more connection with mules than any other place. But the residents here decided there ought to be a monument to the mule someplace and they thought a town named Muleshoe certainly was a logical place. People all over the country contributed money to pay for the monument dedicated at Muleshoe on July 4, 1965.

The early Anglo settlers brought a few mules to Texas. But the big wagons and plows in the early days usually were pulled by oxen. Most of the wagons used to haul buffalo hides from the Plains to Dodge City in the 1870s were pulled by oxen. Mules gradually replaced the oxen because they require less food and water.

Muleshoe was named for the Muleshoe Ranch. This was one of the principal ranches in the area at the time. There were at least three other ranches in other parts of Texas using the Muleshoe brand and name. The custom of branding cattle was handed down by the Spanish. A cattle brand was like a copyright in their system. There were no duplications. Texas made the county clerks responsible for registering brands in 1848. Registration under the Texas system assures the owner exclusive use of his brand only in the counties where he registers it. Somebody else may use the same brand elsewhere in the state.

Bailey County was named for Peter J. Bailey. He was a

Extensive windbreaks have been planted on the Plains since the drought of the 1930s. Most farmhouses are surrounded by evergreens. The trees help keep down dust storms and give some protection from northers.

1

2

The Muleshoe Wildlife Refuge on Farm Road 214 south of Muleshoe is the oldest wildlife refuge in Texas. It was established in 1935 as a haven for migrating waterfowl. Ducks and geese begin arriving here from the north in August. The sandhill cranes usually arrive in September or October. The sandhill cranes stay until about February and there sometimes are 100,000 here. Birdwatchers have recorded sightings of 181 varieties of songbirds at this refuge. The managers of the refuge grow several varieties of grain on the property to feed to the birds.

lawyer from Kentucky and just 24 years old when he was killed by the Mexicans at the Alamo on March 6, 1836.

There have been no significant oil discoveries here yet. The population of about 8,000 is supported mostly by crops and livestock. There are more than 150,000 acres under irrigation in Bailey County.

1) A place called Parmerton was the county seat of Parmer County very briefly but the government moved to Farwell the same year the county was organized. Farwell was named for John V. Farwell and his brother. They were partners in the syndicate that owned the XIT Ranch.
2) The Parmer County Courthouse in Farwell was built in 1916.

PARMER COUNTY

Almost all of this county was included in the original boundaries of the XIT Ranch. Friona and Bovina were originally shipping points for the ranch on the first railroad built through the county. The county seat was named for the managing partner of the syndicate that owned the ranch. Coronado may have passed this way in 1541 looking for those golden cities he never found.

Parmer County was created in 1876. The legislature named it for Martin Parmer. He was one of the early agitators against Mexican rule in Texas. Parmer was born in Virginia. He lived in Tennessee and Missouri and served in the Missouri legislature before he came to Texas the first time in 1826. Parmer joined in Benjamin Edwards' Freedonian Rebellion at Nacogdoches in December of 1826. He fled to Louisiana when the rebellion collapsed in January of 1827. Parmer tried to enter Texas again in 1831. The Mexicans expelled him but he came back again in 1835. He managed to get elected a delegate to the Convention of 1836 and he signed the Declaration of Independence there.

Parmer was often referred to by other pioneers as the "Ringtailed Panther." It is not entirely clear which of his activities earned him this nickname. He was about as devoted to matrimony as he was to revolution. Parmer married five times and fathered at least 16 children before he died in 1850 at the age of seventy-two.

A Texas rancher was probably about the last thing John V. Farwell ever dreamed he would be. He was born in New York

1

2

1) The original bank building in Farwell has been bricked up and annexed to the lawyers' offices next door but it still displays a historical marker. This building is on the square, across the street from the courthouse.

2) The traveler in this part of Texas is never out of sight of grain elevators. The big concrete storage bins are the skyscrapers of the Plains. Every town has one or more and they are visible for miles. This one is in Farwell on the New Mexico state line.

State. His family moved to Illinois while he was still in his teens. John started his career as a bookkeeper for a firm in Chicago. He did well and worked his way up to manager of a dry goods business. Farwell eventually took over the business and he was the leading dry goods merchant in Chicago for a number of years. He was a partner in Taylor, Babcock and Company in 1882 when that company formed the Capitol Syndicate to build the state capitol in Austin in exchange for three million acres of land. The partners in Taylor, Babcock did not know what they were going to do with the land in the beginning. They gave some thought in the early stages to subdividing it. But that would not have recovered the cost of the capitol building for them. The land was worth perhaps 50 cents an acre. They had to find a way to keep the land until they could sell it for more than a dollar an acre because that was about what they had in it. J. Evetts Haley says in his *XIT Ranch of Texas* that A. C. Babcock came down from Chicago and made a personal inspection of the land in 1882. He recommended to his partners that they start a ranch. They agreed and made John Farwell managing partner for the enterprise. He was nearly 60 and a stranger to the cow business. But he came to Texas and ran the ranch until he died in 1908.

The town of Farwell was named for John Farwell and his brother Charles when it was established in 1905 on the New Mexico border. Farwell is at the end of the rail line the Pecos and Northern Texas Railroad extended down into the ranch from Amarillo in 1898.

1

2

1) *The XIT Ranch had a line camp on Catfish Draw in western Parmer County. The first railroad made the camp a shipping point. Cattle milled around the tracks in such numbers that the trains had trouble getting through. The train crews called the place Bulltown. The name was refined to Bovina when the post office was established in 1899. This monument and a marker recall the Bulltown days.*
2) *Friona is the biggest town in Parmer County. It was established by a company the XIT hired to subdivide some of the ranch land. The first church was established on this site in 1909. This adobe building was completed in 1921.*

The census of 1890 showed a population of 70 for Parmer County. All 70 worked for the Capitol Syndicate. The syndicate started selling off some of the XIT land after 1900 and the railroad brought a few settlers in. Real estate promoters were bringing farmers in by 1904. There were 1,700 people in the county by 1920. The population now is about 10,000. Livestock and crops are about equally important in the county's economy today. There are about 400,000 acres of farm land under irrigation. There are more cows in feedlots than there are on the range. No significant oil or gas strikes have been made here so far.

CASTRO COUNTY

The man this county is named for founded several towns in Texas. But none of them is here. Henri Castro's ancestors

The city of Dimmitt was named by and for founder W. C. Dimmitt. It has been the county seat of Castro County since the county government was organized. The present courthouse was built in Dimmitt in 1939.

were Portuguese but he was born in France in 1786. He came to the United States in 1827 and became a naturalized citizen. But he was back in France and working in a Paris bank in 1838 when the Republic of Texas was making one of its periodic efforts to float a loan. Castro tried to be helpful. The loan never was negotiated but Texans appreciated Castro's efforts. Sam Houston made him Paris consul general for the Republic.

Castro parlayed that honorary job into a contract to settle European colonists in Texas. He brought nearly 500 families and more than 450 single men to Texas from France and Germany between 1843 and 1847. He settled them in Medina County where he established the towns of Castroville, Quihi, Vandenburg and D'Hanis.

Castro County was created in 1876 and organized earlier than some of the other counties on the Plains. A few settlers came in during the 1880s. One of them was W. C. Dimmitt. He started a settlement near the center of the county and named it for himself and promoted it. Dimmitt got his town designated the county seat when the county government was organized in 1891.

The first railroad reached the county in 1898. It was the line the Pecos and Northern Texas Company was building from Amarillo to what is now Farwell. This line went through just the northwest corner of Castro County. The town of Summerfield developed there. Exactly comparable developments in several other counties caused county governments to move to the towns on the tracks. But the Castro County government stayed at Dimmitt. The Fort Worth and Denver eventually extended a branch line to Dimmitt, but not until 1926. The town of Hart grew up around the stop that railroad

1

2

1) This old farmstead is the Castro County Museum. It is open weekday afternoons. The museum is in the 400 block of Halsell Street in Dimmitt. Admission is free. There are craft exhibits and demonstrations here during the County Fair in September.

2) The dominant building in the town of Nazareth is the Holy Family Catholic Church. This town was founded on a pleasant hill in eastern Castro County by a few Catholic families in 1902. There have been big changes in the area since then. Ranching has declined. Farming has increased dramatically and most of the cattle are in feed lots.

established on the T. W. Hart Ranch. Nazareth was established in eastern Castro County in 1902 by 15 Catholic families and a priest. But Dimmitt is the principal city and marketplace with about half of the total population of the county.

This is one of the leading agricultural counties in the state with 300,000 acres of farm land under irrigation. Corn is one of the big crops here. There is a corn starch plant in Dimmitt but most of the grain grown here becomes livestock feed. The geologists and seismologists are still looking for the oil and gas in Castro County.

SWISHER COUNTY

The last strongholds of the Comanches were in Tule and Palo Duro canyons. The Palo Duro Canyon begins in Randall County. Tule Canyon begins here in Swisher County and joins the Palo Duro in Briscoe County. There is water and grass in the canyons. The Comanches camped in the canyons regularly and regularly met here with the Comanchero traders. The Comancheros were people, usually of mixed blood, living in New Mexico. They made a business of swap-

1) The late Comanche Chief Quanah Parker probably would approve the vandalizing of this marker.
2) The Swisher County Museum on South Austin at Southeast 3rd Street in Tulia includes a log cabin that was originally a line camp on the JA Ranch.

ping whiskey and guns for the horses the Comanches stole from white settlers.

Ranald Mackenzie tracked the Comanches to their canyon hideouts in 1874 and scattered them. He managed to separate the Indians from their horses and then he had all the horses killed to make sure the Indians did not find them again. Mackenzie's surprise attack on the Comanche camp occurred in Randall County. The Indians' horses were shot in Tule Canyon here in Swisher County in September of 1874. It was almost the end of the road for the Comanches.

The legislature created Swisher County in 1876. Some of the earliest settlers were employees of the JA Ranch founded in 1877 by Charles Goodnight and his rich English partner John Adair. The JA once extended into this county and four other counties. The ranch still exists but it no longer has any holdings in this county. The 1880 census showed a population of only four but there were enough people in Swisher County by 1890 to organize a county government. W. G. Connor donated some of his property near the center of the county for the courthouse and Connor's place was designated the county seat. The settlement that developed was named Tulia for Tule Creek and Tule Canyon. *The Handbook of Texas* says the residents meant to name the town Tullie but somebody in the Post Office Department changed the spelling. It has been Tulia ever since.

The Santa Fe extended a rail line through Swisher County in 1906. Tulia is on the line but the little town of Happy had to move a couple of miles to get on it. Happy is at the north

1   2

*1) The present courthouse in Tulia was built in 1962. Tulia has been the coun-
ty seat of Swisher County since the county was organized in 1890. The town
was named for the principal watercourse in the county. North and Middle
and South Tule draws join in eastern Swisher County to form Tule Creek.
Tule is pronounced "tool."*
*2) The Santa Fe Railroad extended rail service to Tulia in 1906. The railroad
moves only freight here, now, and the depot is vacant.*

edge of the county. The name supposedly is short for "Happy
Hunting Ground."

Swisher County was named for James Gibson Swisher.
Several veterans of the Tennessee Militia helped Tennessee
Militia veteran Sam Houston take Texas away from the Mexicans. Swisher was one of them. He came to Texas in 1833.
He was in Washington County when word reached there that
Mexican troops were trying to reclaim a cannon from the settlers at Gonzales. The Washington County residents raised a
company of volunteers to help the people of Gonzales defend
their cannon. Swisher was elected captain. The people of
Gonzales had already won their skirmish with the Mexicans
by the time Swisher and company reached there. So they went
on to San Antonio and joined in the siege that convinced the
Mexicans to surrender the Alamo. Swisher helped negotiate
the surrender agreement with Mexican General Martin
Perfecto de Cos. He was back in Washington County in time
to be elected a delegate to the Convention of 1836 where he
signed the Declaration of Independence.

Livestock raised on the ranches and in the feedlots here
earn about as much money as the big farms. The livestock
and the crops together earn more than 100 million dollars a
year. There have been no significant oil or gas strikes.

HALE COUNTY

This county was created in 1876 and named for one of the
soldiers killed in Texas' war for independence. John C. Hale
was born in Maine. He came to Texas in 1831 and settled in

85

1

2

1) There were few trees on the Plains when the first settlers came. People have been planting trees ever since and the courthouse lawns in most Plains towns are well shaded today. The courthouse lawn in Plainview also has a number of squirrels. The present Hale County Courthouse was built here in 1910. This is Jimmy Dean's home town.

2) Conrad Hilton had a string of hotels in West Texas before he got into the hotel big league. He sold this one in Plainview many years ago but it still has the Hilton name on it. It is no longer operating as a hotel but it is due to be converted to a retirement home.

what is now Sabine County. He and his neighbor Benjamin Bryant recruited a company of volunteers for the Texas Army in March of 1836. The company joined Sam Houston on March 29th and Hale was serving as a lieutenant of the company when he fell at San Jacinto 23 days later.

The waters of the Ogallala Aquifer are closest to the surface in the High Plains area bounded by Plainview, Lubbock, Muleshoe and Hereford. Some of the first serious irrigation projects were here in Hale County.

The ranchers preceded the farmers here. A family named Morrison from Illinois started the first ranch in the northeast part of the county in 1881. The first settlers came in 1883. Horatio Graves brought his family here and settled on four sections of land in the center of the county that year. He had good luck raising crops and a few other families moved in. They called their community Epworth. The community merged with a settlement called Hale City in 1893 to form the town of Hale Center. Hale Center got rail service in 1909 and it is the second biggest town in Hale County. Abernathy is actually bigger, but it is partly in Lubbock County.

The biggest town in Hale County is Plainview in the northeastern corner of the county. The site was a landmark on the Plains before the first settler came. There were several

1

1) Wayland College was made famous by its women's basketball teams. It is now Wayland University. Gates Hall was built in 1909.
2) The Museum of the Llano Estacado is adjacent to the Wayland campus.

2

hackberry trees in Running Water Draw where the City Park is now. They were the only trees in the area. Z. T. Maxwell settled in the hackberry grove in 1886. He and E. L. Lowe laid out a townsite in 1887. They named their town Plainview and it was designated the county seat when the county government was organized in 1888.

The Santa Fe built a line to Plainview in 1907. This accelerated a land boom that had actually started on the Plains in the late 1800s when the state started offering state lands for sale in tracts of 2,560 acres for $3,200 with $800 down and 40 years on the balance. The land sold quickly and ranchers were inspired to offer some of their land for sale to farmers. Many of the buyers soon went broke because of the drought that began in 1907. The drought increased interest in the underground water.

Promoters brought in a few of the new pumps that had been developed for the rice farms on the coast. They set up demonstration farms to show how much land could be irrigated by the water the new pumps brought up at the rate of 1,000 gallons a minute. Established farmers were slow to pick up on the idea but the promoters made a lot of money selling land to new settlers. Donald E. Green says in his *Land of the*

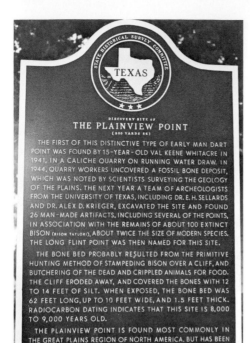

1

1) This marker stands on U.S. Highway 70 at Joliet in a little park. It is a record of an important archaeological discovery that put the name of Plainview in the archaeology textbooks for all time. The excitement subsided a long time ago.
2) The site where the discovery was made is actually part of the Plainview city dump now. The archaeologists know where the bones and artifacts were found and they can return and dig some more if they want to. But it has been some time since there was any digging here. It does not look much like what most people would expect a National Historic Site to look like, but this site is listed in **The National Register of Historic Places.** *Some of the bones and tools found here are on display at the Museum of the Llano Estacado at Wayland University.*

2

Underground Rain that the demonstration wells at Plainview helped the promoters sell five million acres of land between 1910 and 1920 at prices ranging up to $250 an acre. There were several hundred irrigation pumps working on the Plains by 1920. Many farmers were saved by their irrigation systems during the great drought of 1934-35.

Hale County has more than 450,000 acres under irrigation now. The crops earn more than 100 million dollars a year. There is substantial ranching and substantial oil and gas production here, too, but farming likely will continue to be the big business in Hale County as long as the water lasts.

The towns on the Plains promote their high school athletes every way they can. Nearly all of them use the city water towers to advertise and encourage the home team. This is Abernathy's tribute to the Antelopes of Abernathy High. The high school teams compete in other events, too. But it is football that generates the real enthusiasm. The turnouts for the Friday night games here in the fall are the envy of coaches everywhere else. Abernathy is a railroad town. It was established in 1910 on the line the Santa Fe extended that year from Lubbock to Plainview. The town was named for railroad man M. G. Abernathy. Residents of the earlier settlement of Bartonsite moved to Abernathy to get on the rail line. Abernathy is the second biggest town in the county — but part of it is in Lubbock County.

FLOYD COUNTY

The Comanche Indians and the Comanchero traders had a meeting ground in this area before the Comanches were driven off the Plains. The Comanches raided frontier settlements for years and stole cows and horses. They stole more than they needed for themselves and they brought the surplus livestock to the High Plains. Here they traded their surplus to the Comancheros for guns and ammunition and whiskey. The Comancheros brought the guns and ammunition and whiskey here from New Mexico and they took the stolen livestock back and sold it in New Mexico. This trade continued until Ranald Mackenzie broke up the Comanches' camps in the Palo Duro Canyon in the fall of 1874. One of the places the Comanches and the Comancheros met regularly before that was near the base of the Cap Rock on Quitaque Creek here in what is now northeast Floyd County.

Colonel Mackenzie did not know where the Comanches were camped when he came here to put an end to the Indians' depredations. But he knew about the trade between the Indians and the Comancheros and he knew the Comancheros would know where the Indians were. Mackenzie's troops located and captured a Comanchero trader named Jose Tafoya somewhere in this area. The Comanchero told

This was an early horse traders' landmark. Quitaque Peak is an outcrop of the Cap Rock at the eastern edge of Floyd County. The half-breed Comanchero traders from New Mexico brought guns and supplies here to trade for the horses the Comanche Indians stole from the white settlements in Texas. This trade flourished for years until the Comanches were forced off the Plains. The Indians often had big herds of stolen horses here. Quitaque is said to be an Indian word for horse manure. It is pronounced "kittakway."

Mackenzie what he wanted to know. The Colonel apparently made it pretty plain there would be unpleasant consequences if he did not.

The legislature created Floyd County in 1876 and named it for Dolphin W. Floyd. He was one of the men killed defending the Alamo. Floyd went to the mission to join William B. Travis' little garrison just before the final assault. He was one of the "Immortal 32" reinforcements from Gonzales.

The earliest permanent settlers in the county claimed land in Blanco Canyon near the southern county line. Arthur Duncan and his family came first in 1884. Several other families followed the Duncans into the canyon. The first town probably was Della Plain, platted in southern Floyd County by T. J. Braidfoot in 1887. Braidfoot named the town for the daughter of one of his partners and he hoped to make it the county seat. But there were other promoters at work. Several settlers moved from Della Plain to a new site farther north. They started a new town in 1889 and named it Lockney for one of the founders.

Another group started another town and named it Floyd City. So there were three contenders for the county seat when it came time to choose one. That was when the county government was organized in 1890. The people at Lockney threw their support to Floyd City in the election and Floyd City won by 22 votes. There was a court contest but the decision stood. The name of Floyd City was changed to Floydada. Della Plain vanished. Lockney almost did. But J. D. Burleson started the Lockney Christian College there in 1894. The

1

1) *Floydada was named for Floyd County and Mrs. Ada Price. She and her husband had owned the land before the town was established. The present courthouse in Floydada was built in 1923, but it was rebuilt and remodeled extensively after a fire in 1948. Floyd County has the only railroad tunnel still in use in Texas. It is on the Fort Worth and Denver line at the edge of the Cap Rock in the northeast corner of the county.*

2) *The Floyd County Historical Museum is in an old hardware store building on the courthouse square. The museum has a collection of early furnishings, implements and photographs. It is open weekdays and free. There is an Old Settlers' Day here every year on the last Saturday in May.*

3) *Don Hardy builds custom race cars in his shop just off the square in downtown Floydada. Don is a former race driver. Most of the cars he builds in his shop here are dragsters.*

2   3

school drew a number of new people to the town. Lockney almost won the county seat away from Floydada in a second election in 1912. The college closed in 1918 but Lockney still is the second biggest town in the county.

There have been no significant oil or gas discoveries in Floyd County so far. Farming is bigger than ranching. More than 300,000 acres of farmland are under irrigation. Cotton and grains are the most important crops.

1

2

1) Briscoe County was named for Andrew Briscoe. He fought in the revolution and President Sam Houston appointed him the first chief justice of Harrisburg when the republic was established. Briscoe later went into banking and made several attempts to promote railroads.

2) The southwestern half of Briscoe County is on the High Plain. The northeastern half is in the valley of the Prairie Dog Town Fork of the Red River, below the Cap Rock escarpment. Silverton is on the High Plain. The town has been the county seat since Briscoe County was organized in 1892. The present courthouse in Silverton was built in 1922 but it has been altered. The artificial stone trim above the second floor windows is not original.

3) The original jail still stands. It was built of stone from Tule Canyon in 1894. State Highway 207 to the north and State Highway 256 to the east of Silverton are very scenic.

3

BRISCOE COUNTY

This county is on the eastern edge of the High Plains. The western part of the county is high. The eastern part is in the Palo Duro Canyon on the Rolling Plains. The Cap Rock escarpment lies between Silverton and Quitaque.

This was all Comanche country until 1874. The Comanchero trader Jose Tafoya had a trading post near the present town of Quitaque from about 1865 until 1867. He never came near this area again, though, after he told Colonel Ranald Mackenzie in 1874 where Quanah Parker's Comanches had their camp. A ranch established on Quitaque Creek soon after the Indians were flushed out was bought by Charles Good-

TRADING AREA OF JOSE TAFOYA AND OTHER

COMANCHEROS

IN QUITAQUE AREA, COMANCHEROS (PEDDLERS IN COMANCHE DOMAIN) FROM NEW MEXICO TRADED FLOUR AND OTHER GOODS TO INDIANS. THE BARTER (BEGUN IN 1700'S) REACHED PEAK IN 1864-1868, WHEN APACHES, COMANCHE, AND KIOWAS RUSTLED HORSES AND THOUSANDS OF CATTLE "DOWN IN TEXAS", TO USE IN TRADES.

JOSE TAFOYA, WHO HAD WAGONS AS WELL AS PACK MULES, SOLD GUNS TO INDIANS UNTIL U.S. ARMY CAUGHT AND THREATENED TO HANG HIM IN 1874 UNLESS HE ENLISTED AS A FRONTIER SCOUT. THERE WERE MANY OTHER COMANCHEROS. TAFOYA IS AN EXAMPLE OF ONE WHO HELPED RID TEXAS OF INDIAN MARAUDERS.

(1969)

Quitaque Peak is in Floyd County next door but the town of Quitaque is in southeast Briscoe County. Marksmen have been using this marker on State Highway 86, west of town, as a target. The last line in the text on the marker is an interesting example of someone trying to find something to commend in the conduct of a certified scoundrel. What Tafoya did to help rid Texas of Indian marauders was not done in a spirit of helpfulness. It was self-preservation. The successful completion of a wildcat oil well caused some excitement in Briscoe County early in 1982. Marathon Oil made the strike but there was no immediate claim that it was a major find.

night and John Adair in 1882 and made part of their JA Ranch.

There were a few settlers around Quitaque by the late 1880s. The settlement had a population of 30 in 1890 when it became a stage stop. But the newer settlement of Silverton became the county seat when the county government was organized in 1892.

Farmers began to experiment with cotton here fairly early and there was a gin at Quitaque by 1912. The population of the county increased as small farmers moved in. It began to decrease as the small farmers went broke and sold out or abandoned their farms to the mortgage holders. Briscoe County had a population of more than 4,000 in 1940. It is about 2,600 now. There is some irrigation. This is not one of the really big agricultural counties. But farming is more important to the economy than ranching. There have not been any oil or gas discoveries of any consequence in Briscoe County.

The county was named for Andrew Briscoe when the legislature created it in 1876. Briscoe was born in 1810 on his father's plantation in Mississippi. He moved to Texas in 1833 and opened a store at Anahuac. He was arrested by Mexican officials during a dispute over customs duties in 1835 and released through the intervention of William Barret Travis. Briscoe took part in the siege of Bexar in December of 1835. He was a delegate to the Convention of 1836, and he signed

1

1) *Silverton, Tulia, Lockney and Floydada built a dam in Tule Canyon in 1974. The four cities get their water from the reservoir the dam created. A sign at the dam says archaeologists explored the site of Mackenzie Reservoir before it was flooded and found 77 places where humans had lived 10,000 years ago. There are boat ramps, campsites and hookups in a park off State Highway 207. The park is run by a concessionaire. There is an admission fee of $1 per person with extra charges for camping and hookups.*

2) *The fish caught at Mackenzie are mostly crappie and largemouth bass but the Parks and Wildlife Department has been stocking the lake with walleye and smallmouth bass, too. People under 17 and over 65 are exempt but everybody else must have a license to fish in Texas waters. You can get more information free by dialing 1-800-792-1112.*

2

the Declaration of Independence. He was at San Jacinto as an infantry captain. Briscoe made several attempts to promote a railroad in Houston in the 1840s. Then he went into banking. He died in New Orleans in 1849. His widow helped organize the Daughters of the Republic of Texas and she was a charter member of the Texas State Historical Association. Mary Jane Harris Briscoe died in Houston in 1903.

Bones of extinct animals have been found at a number of sites in Briscoe County together with points and tools from the Folsom period so scientists conclude that humans lived here more than 10,000 years ago.

Water conservation projects like the Mackenzie Reservoir, and the irrigation and the windbreaks and contour plowing have reduced the frequency and severity, but the wind still blows on the Plains and there is plenty of loose soil in the cotton fields between seasons so there are some dust storms still. But there have been no scenes recently like this one, photographed during the drought of 1935.

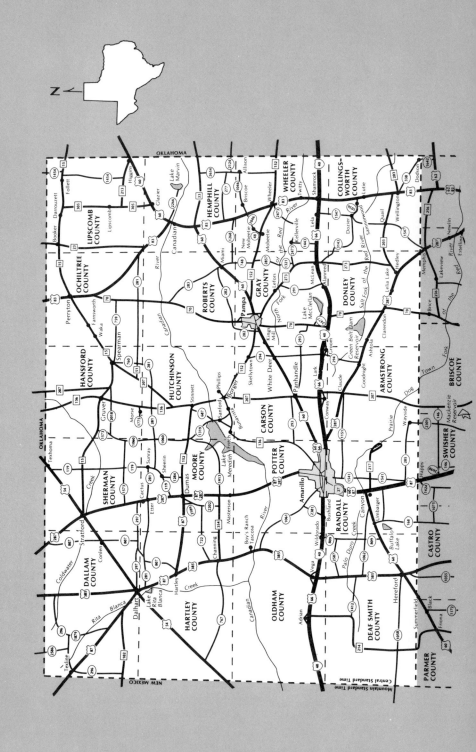

3

Amarillo and the Panhandle

Potter, Oldham, Deaf Smith, Randall,
Armstrong, Donley, Collingsworth,
Wheeler, Hemphill, Lipscomb, Ochiltree,
Roberts, Gray, Carson, Hutchinson,
Hansford, Sherman, Moore, Hartley and
Dallam counties.

The term Panhandle usually refers to a narrow strip of land attached to a larger body, like the Panhandle of Oklahoma or the Panhandle of Florida. The Panhandle of Texas is square. It does not resemble a handle any more than the rest of Texas resembles a pan. But this section of the state has been known as the Panhandle since shortly after the present boundaries were established in 1850.

Most of the Panhandle is on the High Plains. The Ogallala Aquifer extends under most of the counties here. The presence of the underground water and the depth of the valleys in the Canadian River system are evidence that there was more rainfall and more surface water here a few thousand years ago. There is abundant evidence that some kind of humans lived and hunted here 10,000 or 12,000 years ago. They probably were Asians. Their ancestors probably walked across the Bering Straits.

A Pueblo culture flourished in the Panhandle in more recent times. The Pueblo Indians apparently abandoned their stone and adobe villages five or six hundred years ago when the climate became too dry for their primitive agriculture.

The Spanish never had any colonies here. But some of the names are Spanish because Coronado and several other

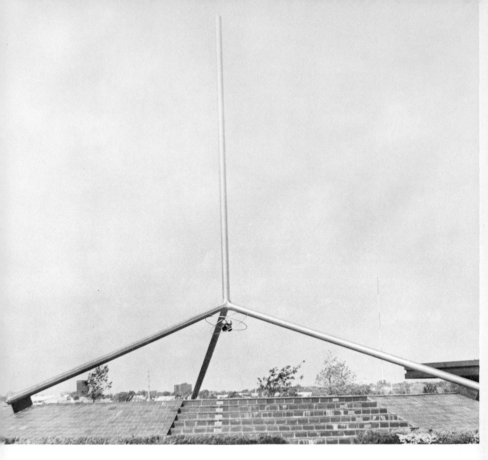

Scientists discovered helium in the gases surrounding the sun in 1868. Traces of the gas were discovered on earth in 1895. Helium was found in the natural gas from wells in the Panhandle in 1918. The first plants to extract helium were established here in 1929. Some of the history of the gas is preserved in a small museum on the Interstate 40 Business Loop in Amarillo. This helium memorial outside the museum is actually four time capsules, one in each leg of the stainless steel monument. The Amarillo Information Center is here in the Helium Museum. Most of the world's helium comes from this area but helium has also been discovered in Wyoming recently. Amarillo is a thriving and busy city. Georgia O'Keefe once taught art here.

Spanish explorers did pass through here and because Mexicans living in the Spanish towns in New Mexico often grazed their sheep here before Texans began to settle in what is now the Texas Panhandle.

POTTER COUNTY

One of the early Anglo travelers in this part of the world was Captain Randolph Marcy of the U.S. Army. He was detailed to escort a big wagon train across Texas in 1849. The

1

2

1) Potter County was named for Robert Potter. He was secretary of the Texas Navy during the revolution. He was killed in the feud between the Regulators and Moderators in East Texas in 1842.

2) The Potter County Courthouse in Amarillo was built in 1931. The main north-south streets in the downtown area are named for presidents of the United States, from Washington through Cleveland

3) The original building of the First Baptist Church of Amarillo looks like new. This little building was moved from its original site to the grounds of the new First Baptist Church at West 12th and South Tyler to be preserved. It was built in 1889.

3

wagon train was made up of people with gold fever. They wanted to get to California the quickest way. Captain Marcy's troops met the wagon train at Fort Smith in Arkansas and guided it to Santa Fe, New Mexico. The party followed the valley of the Canadian River most of the way across what is now the Texas Panhandle. This route was familiar to the Indians and some of the early Spanish travelers had used it. It did not become the main road to California because Marcy found when he reached Santa Fe that there was no decent trail for the gold-seekers to follow on westward from there. He escorted the caravan south to Donna Ana. There was a road from there on west and so Captain Marcy decided he would find a more direct route between Donna Ana and Fort Smith on his way back. He enlisted the help of various Indian guides and marked a trail much farther south, approx-

1) *City founder H. B. Sanborn built this house in 1902. It was originally on another site. It was moved to this lot at West 13th Street and South Madison in 1921. It is a private residence.*

2) *Pioneer cattleman Lee Bivins built this home in 1905 at 1000 Polk Street near downtown Amarillo. Bivins was one of the leaders in the development of the Panhandle oil and gas fields. He was mayor of Amarillo when he died in 1929. His widow left the house to the city when she died in 1951.*

imately through the present cities of Monahans, Odessa, Big Spring, Snyder and Haskell. The first Texas and Pacific rail line across West Texas followed much the same route 32 years later.

Marcy's route across the Panhandle in 1849 brought him through northern Potter County. He was very conscious of his role as a trail blazer and he kept careful notes. He later wrote a couple of books so there is a record of his initial impression of the country around here. What he wrote about the Llano Estacado was that it was a vast, dreary and monotonous waste of barren solitude, "An ocean of desert prairie where the voice of man is seldom heard and where no living being permanently resides." Wags have been paraphrasing Marcy ever since. One of the popular jokes about the Plains is that there is no other place where you can look so far and see so little. These observations are out of date. Millions of Americans and a lot of people elsewhere now depend upon the farmers and ranchers of the Panhandle for food. Amarillo is one of the most important cattle markets in the world. Part of the city is in Randall County,

1

BUILT TO THE GLORIOUS AND PERPETUAL MEMORY OF
FATHER FRAY JUAN DE PADILLA, O. F. M.
FRANCISCAN MISSIONARY,
FIRST MARTYR FOR CHRISTIANITY IN THE
UNITED STATES AND IN TEXAS

ACCOMPANIED THE CORONADO EXPEDITION TO PALO DURO CANYON.
WENT WITH FRANCISCO VASQUEZ DE CORONADO
AND HIS CHOSEN PARTY
IN SEARCH OF LA GRAN QUIVIRA.

RETURNED SOON AND BEGAN HIS ZEALOUS LABORS FOR THE
CIVILIZING AND CHRISTIANIZING
OF THE WICHITA AND OTHER INDIAN NATIONS
IN THE REGION OF THE TEXAS PANHANDLE

HIS MARTYRDOM OCCURRED IN 1544

ERECTED JOINTLY BY THE STATE OF TEXAS
AND THE TEXAS KNIGHTS OF COLUMBUS
IN 1936

2

1) A big engine from the days of steam is on display outside the old Santa Fe depot in Amarillo. Engine Number 5000 was nicknamed "Madame Queen" for a character on the "Amos 'N Andy" radio show.
2) This marker in Ellwood Park honors the memory of the first Christian martyr in our country. Ellwood Park was donated to the city by H. B. Sanborn and named for Sanborn's son.
3) The new Amarillo City Hall and Convention Center were built on eight landscaped blocks near the old railroad depot in 1979.

3

but Amarillo is the county seat of Potter County.

The legislature created this county in 1876 and named it for one of the more mercurial characters involved in our revolution against Mexico. Robert Potter was born in North Carolina. He served two terms in Congress and then spent two years in prison for wounding a couple of other citizens in a dispute. Potter was elected to the North Carolina legislature when he got out of prison but he was expelled when some of his associates took exception to the way he played cards. That happened in 1835 and when it did Potter decided he might as

1) The Amarillo Garden Center is situated in a landscaped valley off Interstate 40 near the Amarillo Medical Center on the west side of town. It is attractive, but the wind is so strong here sometimes it blows the water out of the fountain.

2) The Don Harrington Discovery Center is in the same newly developed area. This is a planetarium and a health and science museum. The exhibition area is open daily. There are public shows on the weekends. The exhibits are free. There is a fee for the shows.

3) The Amarillo Art Center on the Amarillo College campus is open daily except Mondays. It is free.

well move to Texas. He had been a midshipman in the U.S. Navy in his youth so he got himself appointed secretary of the navy in the interim government the Texas Convention of 1836 established after it approved the Declaration of Independence. Potter was a delegate to the convention and a signer of the declaration. He served in the Congress of the Republic until he was killed in the fighting between the Regulators and the Moderators in East Texas in 1842. Potter was aligned with the Moderators in that bloody feud.

The LX Ranch and the Frying Pan Ranch were grazing

1
2

1) The American Quarter Horse Association has the records of all the registered quarter horses in the world. A statue of Wimpy P-1 stands outside the AQHA headquarters in Amarillo. He was the first registered quarter horse, bred by the King Ranch.

2) The Amarillo Livestock Auction Company and the Western Stockyards Company here sell more than 750,000 head of cattle in an average year. There are 150 cattle feed lots within 200 miles of Amarillo and they are capable of handling more than two million head of cattle.

cattle in Potter County by 1881. The first settlement was Wild Horse Lake. Interest in the area increased substantially when the Fort Worth and Denver Railroad approached. A promoter named J. T. Berry learned what the route would be and he filed a claim to a section of land on the route. Berry laid out a townsite and gave it the name Oneida. He intended to make it the county seat and principal shipping point for the county.

Railroad workmen settled temporarily at the site in a cluster of tents they called Ragtown. But the people eligible to vote when the time came to organize a county government and choose a county seat in 1887, were mostly cowboys on the LX Ranch. Fifty-three people voted. Forty-nine of them voted for Oneida. People said it was because Berry offered the LX cowboys two lots apiece for voting his way.

Rancher H. B. Sanborn was unhappy with the outcome. He was one of the owners of the Frying Pan Ranch and the original Texas barbed wire salesman. Sanborn came to Texas in 1875 as an agent for barbed wire inventor J. F. Glidden. Sanborn and Glidden were partners in the ranch and accustomed to having things their way. The railroad passed through Frying Pan property, so Sanborn laid out a townsite beside the tracks on the ranch. He built a hotel fancier than anything in the town that Berry by this time was calling Amarillo. Sanborn offered free lots to anybody interested in moving from Berry's town to his town. He helped pay the moving expenses. The courthouse and the railroad depot were in Berry's town but the business and the population gradually

1

2

1) This was the entrance to Amarillo Air Force Base until the base closed in 1968.
2) The National Park Service conducts tours of the ancient Alibates Flint Quarry at Lake Meredith daily during the summer. "Alibates" is not an Indian word. The quarry was named for a creek named for cowboy Allie Bates.

3

3) An eccentric millionaire named Stanley Marsh has planted a row of old Cadillacs on his ranch outside Amarillo. He considers this art.

moved to Sanborn's town. The two towns were only a mile apart. People started calling Berry's town Old Amarillo and Sanborn's town New Amarillo. The word "amarillo" is Spanish for yellow. A lake and a creek here had been called Amarillo before the towns were established.

Sanborn managed to get the railroad to stop at his town as well as at the depot in Berry's town. He had about everything then except the county seat and he got the county seat in an election in 1903.

Ranching still is bigger than farming in this county. The first oil strike was in 1925 and there has been substantial oil and gas production here ever since. Most of the world's known reserves of helium are in the immediate vicinity.

1

1) *The leading cause of death in our frontier towns was homicide. The victims died "with their boots on" and they were buried in cemeteries often called "Boot Hill." The Boot Hill Cemetery at old Tascosa is carefully preserved. It is just off U.S. 385.*

2) *Tascosa was the county seat when Oldham County was first organized. This was the courthouse from 1884 until the government moved to Vega. Rancher Julian Bivins donated the courthouse and town site to the Cal Furley Boys' Ranch in 1939.*

2

OLDHAM COUNTY

The first real town in the Panhandle was here in what is now Oldham County. Tascosa was established before the legislature divided this area into counties in 1876. There was some traffic through here long before there was a town. What trade there was between the settlements in New Mexico and those in Louisiana moved usually through the valley of the Canadian.

A Mexican teamster supposedly gave the name Atascosa to one of the creeks feeding into the Canadian because "atascosa" means "boggy" and that's the kind of place it was. A few Mexican sheepherders settled near the mouth of this creek and their settlement was called Atascosa until people began shortening it to Tascosa. The adobe town was 300 miles beyond the Texas frontier settlements when the cattle drivers first started using the Western Trail to the Kansas markets. The cattle drivers made Tascosa a regular stop. The town was also the principal way station on the early road between Dodge City and the settlements in New Mexico. It was the only town in the area when the first ranches were

THE HISTORIC LS
[HEADQUARTERS 6 MILES SOUTHEAST]

GREAT EARLY RANCH WELL KNOWN TO BADMAN BILLY THE KID AND OTHER FAMED WESTERN CHARACTERS, THE LS WAS FOUNDED IN 1870'S BY FORMER INDIAN TERRITORY TRADER W. M. D. LEE, AND NEW YORK FINANCIER LUCIEN SCOTT. THROUGH LEE'S EFFORTS, THE LS HAD WATER AND GRASS FOR OVER 100,000 CATTLE AND SOMETIMES DROVE 6 OR 7 HERDS A YEAR UP THE TRAIL. WHEN THEFTS FOLLOWED BILLY THE KID'S VISITS, LS MEN RODE WEST AND BROUGHT BACK THEIR CATTLE; AND WHEN TASCOSA GUNFIGHTS PUT MEN INTO BOOT HILL GRAVES, THE LS ESCAPED DISASTER. BUT DROUTH BROUGHT HEAVY LOSSES IN 1886; AND GRANT OF 3,000,000 ACRES OF PANHANDLE LANDS TO THE XIT (STATE OF TEXAS' PAYMENT FOR CONSTRUCTING CAPITOL IN AUSTIN) CUT OLD LS RANGE IN HALF. LEE LEFT IN 1890 TO PROMOTE A SHIP CANAL IN HOUSTON. SCOTT DIED 1893; W. H. GRAY AND E. F. SWIFT OF CHICAGO BOUGHT LS IN 1905.

MEMORABLE LS MEN INCLUDED FOREMAN J. E. MCALISTER, LATER A CHANNING MERCHANT. ONE OF THE $25-A-MONTH COWBOYS WAS E. L. DOHENY, LATER A MULTI-MILLIONAIRE OIL MAN INVOLVED IN 1920'S TEAPOT DOME SCANDAL.

OWNERSHIP OF BRAND AND 96,000 ACRES OF LS RANGE PASSED TO COL. C. T. HERRING, RANCHER AND CIVIC LEADER OF AMARILLO; HIS ESTATE STILL OPERATES IT.

1

2

1) This marker on U.S. 385 near the Canadian River crossing recalls some of the history of one of the famous ranches of the Tascosa area.
2) Cal Farley's Boys' Ranch has been caring for homeless and delinquent boys since 1939. The ranch has its own brand and its own cows and plenty of willing cowboys.

established. The XIT, LIT, LX, LS and Frying Pan ranches all got their supplies through Tascosa at one time.

Tascosa was being called the cowboy capital in those days. Billy the Kid and Pat Garrett were among the frontier personalities frequenting Tascosa's saloons during the town's heyday. The queen of the place was a lady known as Frenchy McCormick. It was not her real name and she never told anybody what her real name was. But she did claim she was a Creole from Louisiana and an actress before she married Mickey McCormick. Mickey was the proprietor of a popular saloon and gambling house in the cowboy town. Frenchy became his monte dealer and everybody's darling.

The first railroad in the county missed Tascosa. The trail drives had ended by then and Tascosa was no longer a place of any importance. It had been designated the county seat when the county government was organized in 1880. But the county government moved to Vega in 1915. There were only 15 people still living in Tascosa by that time. Frenchy McCormick was one of them. Mickey's saloon had folded in the late 1880s. Mickey died in 1908. But Frenchy lived on alone in the ghost town until 1939. She moved to Channing then and died two years later.

Vega was established by P. H. Landergrin and John Landergrin in 1906 on the Chicago, Rock Island and Gulf Railroad line. It has not grown very much. The population is under 1,000 but Vega is the principal town in the county. Ranching is still the chief enterprise in Oldham County but there is some farming, too. Oil was discovered in 1957 but Oldham County is not one of the big oil counties.

The present Oldham County Courthouse was built when the government moved from Tascosa to Vega in 1915. Some of the store buildings here are older. Vega is a Spanish word. It means "grassy plain" and it takes the Spanish pronunciation here, VAY-guh.

This county was named for Williamson S. Oldham. He was born in Tennessee and he lived in Arkansas for a while before he moved to Texas in 1849. Oldham ran for the legislature and for Congress while he was in Arkansas. He ran for the legislature in Texas. He lost all of those races but he did serve as a member of the Confederate Senate during the Civil War. He and a committee of other senators reported to President Jefferson Davis in 1864 that the South had the resources to carry on for another 10 years. Oldham moved to Mexico when the South collapsed the following year. A number of devout Confederates did that but most found the Mexicans did not appreciate them as much as they had expected. Oldham returned to Texas in 1866. He died in Houston in 1868.

DEAF SMITH COUNTY

This is one of the areas where the waters of the Ogallala Aquifer are close to the surface. Almost 500,000 acres of farmland are under irrigation in Deaf Smith County. It is one of the richest agricultural counties in the state. The big crops are feed grains. Much of the grain is fed to cattle in the big feedlots and the cattle actually are the biggest money makers in the county. Substantial crops of cotton, vegetables and sugar beets are grown in Deaf Smith County, too. There is a sugar mill on the western outskirts of Hereford. The experiments with irrigation started here in 1910, about the same time they started in Plainview. The livestock and crops in this county earn more than 200,000,000 dollars a year.

Deaf Smith County was created by the legislature in 1876 and named for Erastus Smith. He was the Texas Army scout known as Deaf Smith. He was born in New York in 1787. He came to Texas in 1821 and settled near San Antonio. He married a Mexican woman and they had several children before the revolution began in 1835. Smith had many friends on both

1

2

TOWN WITHOUT A TOOTHACHE

HEREFORD'S "MIRACLE WATER" WAS
BROUGHT TO NATIONAL FAME IN 1941
WHEN DR. EDWARD TAYLOR, STATE
DENTAL OFFICER, TOLD THE AMERICAN
DENTAL ASSOCIATION THAT TOOTH
DECAY WAS ALMOST UNKNOWN HERE.

THIS IDEAL SITUATION HAD BEEN
DISCOVERED BY A LOCAL DENTIST,
DR. GEORGE HEARD, ORIGINALLY FROM
ALABAMA, IN A CROSS-SECTION
SURVEY, DENTISTS FOUND THAT FEW
LOCAL PEOPLE HAD DENTAL CAVITIES.
HEREFORD'S MINERAL-RICH WATER
AND SOIL ARE THOUGHT TO PREVENT
TOOTH DECAY.

DEMAND AROSE FOR HEREFORD
WATER TO BE SHIPPED ALL OVER
THE U.S. AND TO FOREIGN NATIONS.
(1967)

3

1) This county was named for the ablest scout employed by the Texas Army during the revolution. Erastus Smith had difficulty hearing. Disabilities usually became nicknames on the frontier and Erastus was known as Deaf Smith. He had been in Texas longer than most of the soldiers in the Texas Army and he knew the Mexicans well. He saved the day for the Texans more than once.

2) This is a very prosperous county and the people of the county must have been feeling especially prosperous in 1910 when they built their courthouse in Hereford. The entire exterior is faced with marble.

3) The idea of adding flouride to drinking water probably started here in Deaf Smith County. This mineral and other minerals occur naturally in the well water here and people here rarely have problems with their teeth. The minerals are not an unmitigated blessing. They discolor some people's teeth sometimes.

sides and he tried to be neutral when the fighting started. But the Mexican soldiers in San Antonio treated him like a Texan so he joined our side. He knew the country better than most of the Texas soldiers and he performed several valuable services for the rebels before he performed the one that got in all the history books. Deaf Smith destroyed Vince's Bridge at San Jacinto on Sam Houston's orders so there could be no retreat by either side from the battlefield where Texas' fate was decided the afternoon of April 21, 1836. Smith was nearly 50 when he did that. He died a little over a year later at Richmond.

Most of the people in Deaf Smith County live in the vicinity of Hereford, now. But the poplation was scattered among a few cow camps in the beginning. A few big ranches held most of the area when the county was created. The T Anchor was one of the earliest. A large part of the county was included in the original boundaries of the XIT Ranch in 1882. The XIT and several other pioneer ranches in the Panhandle were importing purebred Hereford bulls by 1884 to upgrade their herds. The Hereford breed was developed in England

1

2

3

4

1) The white faced cows Hereford was named for are still here in big numbers, but more often in feedlots than on the range, now.

2) The house rancher E. B. Black built at 508 West 3rd Street is now a museum, open Sunday afternoons and on special occasions.

3) The National Cowgirl Hall of Fame Museum is in the Deaf Smith County Library building on the courthouse square. It is open daily except Sundays. An all-girl rodeo is held here the second weekend in May.

4) The Deaf Smith County Historical Museum has pioneer relics on display indoors and out, at 400 Sampson, across from the courthouse.

5) Most of the towns on the Plains still have some of the red brick streets that were common everywhere in Texas in the 1920s and 1930s. Hereford still has a 1930's flexible stop sign at one intersection on the square.

5

This marker on U.S. 60 east of Hereford attests that Texas cowboys were not always contented with their lot. The gun battle at Tascosa occurred in March of 1886. It lasted only five minutes but left four men dead.

SITE OF
GREAT COWBOY STRIKE
(3 MILES SOUTH)

BEGAN IN SPRING OF 1883 WHEN RANGE HANDS FROM LS, LX, LIT AND OTHER LARGE RANCHES ORGANIZED A STRIKE FOR BETTER WAGES. WAS A REACTION TO LOSS OF PRIVILEGES GIVEN EARLIER AND TO ATTITUDE OF BIG LAND OWNERS TOWARD COWBOYS.

SEVERAL HIRED HANDS GATHERED AT ALAMOCITOS, HEADQUARTERS OF LS, TO PROTEST. MEN ON EVERY RANCH SOON ASKED FOR HIGHER PAY, BUT STRIKE FAILED DUE TO SURPLUS OF COWBOYS AND NO MEANS TO ENFORCE DEMANDS.

STRIKE GAVE FORCE TO LITTLE MEN OPPOSING CATTLE BARONS AND THREE YEARS LATER ERUPTED IN TASCOSA INTO ONE OF THE BLOODIEST GUN FIGHTS THE WEST HAD EVER SEEN.

sometime in the 1700s. Herefords adapted quickly to the Texas Plains. They were good at foraging for themselves. They matured quickly and held their weight pretty well on the drives to market. They were popular. So, when a little settlement developed in the southeast corner of this county about 1880, the settlers named it for the cows.

Hereford was designated the county seat when the county government was organized in 1890. The Panhandle and Santa Fe Railroad reached Hereford the same year. It has been the county seat and principal town in Deaf Smith County since that time. The first farmers began moving into the area when the railroads and ranches started selling off their lands around 1900. Hereford has a population of more than 14,000 now, and it is prosperous. Farming and ranching have made it so. No oil or gas discoveries of any consequence have been made here yet.

RANDALL COUNTY

The most spectacular scenery and one of the most important historic sites in the Panhandle are in the Palo Duro Canyon State Park here in Randall County.

Randall County is on the High Plains. But a tributary of the Prairie Dog Town Fork of the Red River has cut a canyon down to the level of the Rolling Plains. The Palo Duro Canyon begins abruptly in western Randall County. The canyon widens as it passes through Armstrong and Briscoe counties into Hall County. It is narrow at the upper end here in Randall County. Most of the Randall County part of the canyon is included in the Palo Duro Canyon State Park. This is the biggest state park in Texas.

It was near the southeast corner of what is now the state park that Colonel Ranald Mackenzie and his troops surprised Quanah Parker's Indians in the fall of 1874. General William T. Sherman had given Mackenzie orders in 1871 to rid Texas

110

1

2

1) The Randall County Courthouse in Canyon was built in 1909. The city of Canyon grew out of the headquarters of the T-Anchor Ranch, established here in 1878 by Jot Gunter and William Munson.

2) L. T. Lester built this home in Canyon in 1904. Lester came to the Panhandle to hunt buffalo and he stayed to become the first banker in Canyon. The Lester house is on 4th Avenue at 8th Street.

3) The early Texas legislatures were fairly careless about spelling. Several of our counties have names not spelled the same way the people they were named for spelled their names. Randall County was named for Horace Randal.

3

of the Plains Indians, Mackenzie had to catch them first and it took him a while. Many of the Indians responsible for the raids that caused Sherman to start this campaign were supposed to be living on reservations in Oklahoma. Quanah Parker's band of Quahadi Comanches never had agreed to settle on the reservation. One of Mackenzie's objectives was to see that they did. He tracked the Quahadis to the Panhandle where he knew they must have a winter campground. He found a Comanchero trader and forced him to divulge the location of the campground.

Mackenzie's mounted troopers surprised the Indians in their snug camp on the floor of the Palo Duro at dawn on the 28th of September. The soldiers stampeded the Indians' horses first because no one wanted to try to deal with mounted Comanches. The Indian braves were caught at a serious disadvantage but they put up a fight until their women and children could escape. Then they fled the camp, too. The soldiers did not pursue them. They methodically destroyed all

1

2

1) *West Texas State University started as West Texas Normal College in 1910. The school's campus in Canyon once was part of the T-Anchor Ranch. The name of the school was changed to West Texas State Teachers' College in 1923. It became West Texas State College in 1949 and a university in 1963.*

2) *The Panhandle-Plains Historical Society built the Pioneer Hall Museum on the West Texas campus in 1932. The museum is open weekdays and on Sunday afternoons. There is no fee.*

3) *There are major exhibits here on geology, paleontology and natural history, pioneer furnishings and Indian artifacts like this Comanche headdress.*

4) *An original log building from the old T-Anchor Ranch is displayed behind a sturdy fence on the grounds outside this outstanding museum.*

3

4

1) Park Road 5, off State Highway 217, east of Canyon leads into Palo Duro Canyon and the biggest of the Texas State Parks.
2) There are miles of scenic trails and 116 campsites in Palo Duro Canyon State Park. It is a Class I park with the usual fees. Coronado passed this way when he was investigating rumors about golden cities.

the provisions and equipment and tepees in the camp and later killed all the Indians' horses. The Comanches and the few Kiowas and Cheyennes allied with them were left on foot without food or shelter. They split up into small groups and stayed on the move but the soldiers harassed them through the winter until they began to give up. The Kiowas showed up at Fort Sill to surrender in February. The Cheyennes gave up in March. Quanah Parker and the surviving Quahadis gave up in June, 1875.

The first ranch in the Panhandle was in the Palo Duro Canyon. Charles Goodnight established it the year after Mackenzie cleared the Indians out. Goodnight had been ranching for years in Palo Pinto County and in New Mexico and Colorado. He brought a herd of Durham cattle down from Colorado and set up headquarters in a dugout in the canyon a year before he and John Adair founded the JA Ranch farther down the canyon.

Jot Gunter and William Munson established the T Anchor Ranch in the center of Randall County in 1878. The ranch headquarters were where the city of Canyon is today. L.G. Conner started the settlement at the site. It was first called Canyon City. Canyon was designated the county seat when the county government was organized in 1889. It was named for the Palo Duro Canyon.

Randall County was named for Horace Randal. It was another case of good intentions compromised by bad spelling in Austin. Randal was born in Tennessee and his parents

The musical pageant "Texas" is staged in the spectacular amphitheater in the Palo Duro Park nightly except Sundays during the summer. There is a separate fee for admission to the pageant.

brought him to Texas in 1839 when he was six years old. He went to the U.S. Military Academy and served several years with the U.S. Army on the Texas frontier. He switched to the Confederate Army when Texas seceded from the Union in 1861. Randal was commanding a Confederate brigade when he was killed at the battle of Jenkins' Ferry in Arkansas in 1864.

There is some irrigated farming in Randall County but ranching is still more important to the economy here. No significant deposits of oil or gas have been found in Randall County.

ARMSTRONG COUNTY

Ranching has been the chief enterprise in Armstrong County since the county was created in 1876. The first ranch here was the JA and it is the biggest today.

Jot Gunter and William B. Munson probably were the first real estate operators in this part of the world. Both men were lawyers and they formed a partnership in 1878 to buy land certificates and locate land claims in the Texas Panhandle. They were the people Charles Goodnight went to see when he and John Adair decided to start the JA Ranch.

Gunter and Munson agreed to sell the JA partners 12,000 acres and they let Goodnight pick the land. His selection included most of the best waterholes in the Palo Duro Canyon. Goodnight had been a cowman and a trail driver for more than 20 years by this time and he knew well what he was doing. Adair was an Englishman with money. He lent Goodnight enough to permit him to buy a third interest in the JA. Goodnight was the manager of the JA for the first ten years. Adair died in 1885. His heirs bought Goodnight's interest in

1

1) *The cars and trucks are later models and the gasoline is much more expensive, but nothing else has changed very much on the town square at Claude since the Hollywood people were here making* **Hud** *from Larry McMurtry's 1961 novel,* **Horseman, Pass By.**

2) *The Armstrong County Courthouse was built in Claude in 1912. There was a copper trim originally where the simulated stone is now, above the third floor windows.*

3) *The homey county jail building looks older than it is. The county demolished an old jail built in 1894 and used the same stones to build this one in 1953.*

2   3

the ranch in the Palo Duro and sold him another ranch. Goodnight later sold that ranch but he continued to operate a smaller ranch at Goodnight, here in Armstrong County, until he died in 1929.

The JA Ranch spread over more than one million acres and extended into five other counties at one time in the early 1900s. It is smaller today but still a major ranch, still in the Adair family and still managed from the original headquarters in the canyon in southeast Armstrong County.

It is not clear which Armstrong the legislature was honoring in the naming of this county. The historical marker on the

1

2

1) The JA Ranch is off Ranch Road 2272 in southeastern Armstrong County. Some of the buildings at the ranch headquarters were built in the 1880s while Charles Goodnight was still managing the JA. The present main house was built onto the original log headquarters house.

2) The JA is smaller than it was but it is still owned by descendants of original owner John Adair. The big ranch is managed by Monty Richie. He is a grandson of the Adairs. Richie is in his 80s but he was still taking a personal hand in working the cows in the fall of 1981.

3) Pioneer cattleman Charles Goodnight settled on a small ranch at Goodnight after he sold his minority interest in the JA in 1887.

4) There still are some real cowboys in the Panhandle, doing their work the way cowboys always have. These work for the Figure 3 Ranch in Armstrong County.

3

4

courthouse lawn and *The Handbook of Texas* both say the county was named for Texas pioneers by the name of Armstrong. There was a James Armstrong in the Congress of the Republic where he worked on the annexation treaty. And Major John B. Armstrong served with the Texas Rangers and founded the Armstrong Ranch in Willacy County.

The settlement that became the town of Claude was named for a locomotive engineer. The settlement developed when the Fort Worth and Denver Railroad laid its tracks through Arm-

FIRST BATTLE OF THE
PALO DURO
(AUG. 30, 1874)

OPENING FIGHT IN 1874-75 U. S.
ACTION AGAINST TRIBES SUPPOSEDLY
ON INDIAN TERRITORY RESERVATIONS
(PRESENT OKLAHOMA), BUT ACTUALLY
OCCUPYING THE TEXAS PANHANDLE.
SOUTH FROM FORT DODGE, KANS.,
MARCHED 750 SOLDIERS UNDER GEN.
NELSON A. MILES, WHO ON AUG. 28 HAD
TO LEAVE GUARDS WITH HIS STALLED
SUPPLY TRAIN. ATTACKED ON AUG. 30
IN RUGGED TERRAIN BY SUPERIOR
NUMBERS OF CHEYENNES, COMANCHES,
AND KIOWAS, MILES WON VICTORY IN
5-HOUR FIGHT AT BATTLE CREEK (10
MI. E OF HERE) — FIRST OF 14 FIGHTS
IN RED RIVER WAR THAT BROKE THE
INDIANS' POWER IN TEXAS PANHANDLE.
(1971)

This marker looks like it might have been here when the soldiers and the Indians were shooting at each other. The bullet holes are from a more recent but no more civilized time. The information on this marker does not add a lot to the story of the final showdown between the army and the Plains Indians. But it is worth a stop because of its location. The marker is in a little roadside park perched on the edge of the Cap Rock overlooking Palo Duro Canyon. The park is on State Highway 207, about 25 miles south of Claude. Highway 207 is one of the more scenic drives in this area.

strong County in 1887. Claude Ayers was the engineer on the first train that reached here after the track was finished. Claude was designated the county seat when the county government was organized in 1890. A few farmers moved into Armstrong County when the railroad came through and there is substantial farming in the county today. But it is not as important to the county's economy as ranching. There have been no oil or gas strikes here yet.

DONLEY COUNTY

This county originally had another name. The legislature named it Wegefarth County when it was first created in 1873. There had been no development by 1876 when the legislature approved the law creating most of the present Panhandle counties. This county was re-named in that legislation. Wegefarth was an officer of the Texas Immigrant Aid and Supply Company. The present name honors Stockton P. Donley. He was a justice of the Texas Supreme Court. He was elected to that office at the end of the Civil War. U.S. occupation authorities removed him and most of the other officials elected in 1866 because they had been officers in the Confederate Army. Many of the Texas officials the U.S. Army deposed resumed their political careers after Reconstruction ended. Chief Justice Oran Roberts was removed from the supreme court at the same time Donley was. Roberts later was elected governor and he was serving as governor when his county finally was organized in 1882. But Donley died in 1871 before the carpetbaggers lost control of the state.

Cattlemen began moving into Donley County in the late

1

1) *Most of the Plains area looked like this 50 years ago. Scenes like this one in Donley County will become more common again if some new source of water is not found before the ground water runs out. Donley County was not blessed with a lot of ground water.*

2) *The Donley County Courthouse in Clarendon was built in 1890. It needs some repairs. Chances are when it gets them it will get aluminum windows, too.*

3) *St. John the Baptist Episcopal Church was built in Clarendon in 1893. This is said to be the oldest church building continuously in use in the Panhandle.*

2

3

1870s. One of the first settlements in the county was established by Methodist minister Lewis Henry Carhart. He was living in Sherman and preaching there when he got interested in helping people settle in the Panhandle. The main reason for his interest was his concern that there were not enough of the right kind of people in the Panhandle. Carhart advertised for immigrants and led a small group of church members to Donley County in 1878. They settled on the Salt Fork of the Red River and called the place Clarendon for Carhart's wife, Clara. The cowboys were conscious of what the people at

1

1) *A school the Methodists called Allentown Academy when they founded it in the original town of Clarendon moved to New Clarendon in 1898 and became Clarendon College. Clarendon College closed in 1927 and Clarendon Junior College opened on the same hilltop site in 1928.*

2) *Clarendon and four other cities formed the Greenbelt Water Authority to develop a municipal water supply. The authority built Greenbelt Reservoir on the Salt Fork of the Red River and it has become a major recreation center for people in this area. There are boat ramps at each end of the dam. There is a small fee for using them. Trailer hookups and campsites are also available. The site of the original town of Clarendon is now at the bottom of this reservoir. The big event in Clarendon is the July Fourth celebration with a rodeo and a fiddlers' contest.*

2

Clarendon thought about them and they called Claredon "Saints' Roost." Clarendon became the county seat in 1882 and then moved a few years later. The Fort Worth and Denver Railroad built its tracks a few miles south of the original townsite. Clarendon moved to the tracks. It is still the county seat and principal town in Donley County. Carhart had already moved away before his town moved and he kept moving. He went into ranching and he ran a bath house for a while. He lived in England and in Arkansas before he died in California in 1891. He was a cousin of John Wesley Carhart, the inventor of the automobile.

Gas was discovered in Donley County in 1967. No oil has been found here yet. There is some farming but most of the income is from livestock.

COLLINGSWORTH COUNTY

This county was named for one of the Texas heroes from Tennessee but a couple of the towns were named for noble subjects of the British crown. The county was named for James Collinsworth. He arrived in Texas in 1835 and joined immediately in the agitation for separation from Mexico. Collinsworth was elected a delegate to the Convention of

Britain was still the world's banker in the 1880s and 1890s and wealthy Englishmen had a lot of money invested in Texas ranches. Some of them owned a big ranch here and they named the town of Wellington for the English hero Arthur Wellesley, Duke of Wellington. The town was established 75 years after the duke led an Allied army to a decisive victory over Napoleon at Waterloo in 1815.

1836. He signed the Declaration of Independence and he nominated Sam Houston of Tennessee to be commander-in-chief of the Texas Army. Houston made Collinsworth a major in his army and gave him a commendation for his conduct at San Jacinto. Collinsworth was the first chief justice of the Supreme Court of the Republic of Texas. He was a candidate for president when he drowned himself in Galveston Bay in 1838. The legislature spelled his name wrong when it created this county in 1876.

Collingsworth County is on the Oklahoma border but Texans didn't know it until years after the county was created. Texas originally claimed a big part of what is now western Oklahoma. The Texas legislature designated part of that Oklahoma territory as Greer County in 1860. People living there thought they were Texans until the U.S. Supreme Court resolved the issue in 1906 and put the state boundary where it is now.

The pattern of development here was similar to that in the other Panhandle counties. There were a few buffalo hunters first and then cattlemen and then farmers. There were bad feelings here in the early days between the cowmen and the small farmers the cowmen called nesters. The tension caused some people to refer to Collingsworth County as "Killingsworth County" for a time. The disagreements were not all over fences. There was a little settlement named Pearl that was probably the logical place for the county seat when the county was organized in 1890. But the foreman of the Rocking Chair Ranch rounded up enough cowboys to outvote the settlers at Pearl when the election was held. A site named Wellington on the Rocking Chair property was designated the county seat. It was not a town but it soon became one. The saloon keeper at Pearl lost no time moving his business and his building to Wellington. But he didn't make a big killing.

1   2

1) The present Collingsworth County Courthouse was built in Wellington in 1931. The population of the county is under 5,000. About two-thirds of the people in the county live in Wellington.

2) The small Collingsworth County Historical Museum at 1404 15th Street is open Sunday afternoons. There is no fee.

3) The campground in Pioneers' Park on U.S. 83 north of Wellington is free but campers using the hookups are expected to pay a $2 fee, on the honor system.

3

The county voted dry in 1898. It was one of the first counties in Texas to adopt prohibition.

Wellington was named for England's Duke of Wellington because a relative of one of the owners of the Rocking Chair Ranch had been at Waterloo with the duke. The Earl of Aberdeen was one of the owners of the Rocking Chair and the settlement of Aberdeen in the northeast corner of Collingsworth County was named for him. The townsite was part of the ranch at the time.

The Rocking Chair Ranch was located originally in the Hill Country. John Dickerson and Wiley Dickerson moved their herd and the brand to this county in 1880. They sold out in 1881. The buyers later sold the brand and 150,000 acres to an

Bonnie Parker and Clyde Barrow caused some excitement here during the crime spree that ended when lawmen shot them both to death in 1934. Bonnie and Clyde were the most notorious desperadoes in this part of the country in the middle '30s. They were also folk heroes. People blamed them for things they never did and reported seeing them in places they never were. Their legend was bigger than the facts but the facts were deadly enough. They murdered at least 12 people.

Englishman and he sold out in 1883 to a syndicate of Scottish noblemen. The Scots formed a corporation they called the Rocking Chair Ranche Company, Limited. The managers they sent over to run the ranch did not do very well at it. The ranch lost money and the Scots sold it in 1896.

The first railroad reached Wellington in 1910. Oil was discovered in 1936 in very modest quantities. Farming ranks ahead of livestock in earnings here now.

WHEELER COUNTY

There were white buffalo hunters on these Plains well before Ranald Mackenzie and the U.S. Army cleared out the last of the Comanches. This was one reason the Comanches acted the way they did. David Dary says in his *Buffalo Book* that the systematic slaughter of the buffalo began in the summer of 1872 in Kansas and Nebraska after leather workers in the eastern United States and Europe discovered the hides worked up about as well as cow hides. There were buffalo hunters' camps in the Texas Panhandle before the end of that year. One of the early camps was at the head of Sweetwater Creek in what is now northern Wheeler County. It was called Hidetown. Several other buffalo camps had the same name. The hunters in this one provided their own protection in the beginning. They were way beyond the line of frontier forts. But the army garrison at Fort Sill established an outpost near Hidetown in 1875. Fort Elliott was the last fort the army built on the Indian frontier.

Little action occured at Fort Elliott. The Comanches had been demoralized shortly before the fort was built. But the

1

2

1) Wheeler County was the first county in the Panhandle to organize a government and this was the first county seat. The town of Mobeetie grew up near the army's Fort Elliott. The fort was built of wood and adobe and the only remnant of it left is the crude flagpole here in front of the old Wheeler County jail at Old Mobeetie. The old jail is now a museum. It is open daily. There is no fee but donations are welcome.

2) The railroad missed Mobeetie. Most of the people moved to the tracks and started a town they called New Mobeetie. A few people still live at Old Mobeetie but many of the houses are abandoned and falling down.

ranchers and settlers were not yet sure the Indians would not come back. So they built their homes near the fort in a settlement they called Sweetwater. The settlement survived when the buffalo hunters finished their work and left. The legislature created Wheeler County in 1876 and the county was the first one in the Panhandle to organize a county government. The election was held in 1879 and the settlement on Sweetwater Creek was designated the county seat. The settlement applied for a post office and the Post Office Department sent back word that the name would have to be changed. The town in Nolan County had already claimed Sweetwater. So the Wheeler County seat was re-named Mobeetie. It is written in several places that this is an Indian word meaning sweet water. There is another story that the word means buffalo manure.

Mobeetie became an important town. The courthouse at Mobeetie was the first one in the Panhandle and Wheeler County officials looked after the affairs of 14 other counties until those counties completed their organization and built courthouses.

The army abandoned Fort Elliott in 1890. A storm damaged some of the buildings in Mobeetie in 1898. A new settlement named Wheeler was attracting settlers by this time. Wheeler was near the center of the county and the people of

1

2

1) This building was the Wheeler County jail for 16 years. The county government moved from Mobeetie to Wheeler in 1907. The frame courthouse was moved, too. But the stone jail at Mobeetie was not portable. This new jail was built in Wheeler in 1909. The building housed the Wheeler County Museum for a time after it ceased to be used as a jail. It now houses some county offices. The museum exhibits have been moved to the Pioneer West Museum in Shamrock.

2) The present Wheeler County Courthouse in Wheeler was built in 1925. It is on U.S. 83 but U.S. 83 has another name within the city limits of Wheeler. It is called Alan Bean Street because this is the astronaut's home town.

Wheeler eventually promoted an election to move the county seat. They won and the county government moved to Wheeler in 1907. Wheeler has been the county seat since then.

Mobeetie suffered another setback in 1929 when the Panhandle and Santa Fe Railroad built a line across the north end of the county that missed Mobeetie by a couple of miles. Most of the businesses moved to the railroad. The settlement there was named New Mobeetie and Mobeetie became Old Mobeetie. There are people still living in both towns but neither town is thriving. The biggest town in the county is Shamrock but it is not as lively as it was before Interstate Highway 40 drew most of the traffic off old Route 66. The population of Wheeler County peaked at 15,000 in 1930. It is just over 6,000 now. Oil was discovered here in 1921 and there is substantial production. Ranching is bigger than farming but the oil and gas earn more than twice as much as agriculture here.

Wheeler and Wheeler County were named for Royal T. Wheeler. He was born in Vermont and he lived in Ohio and Arkansas before he came to Texas in 1839. Wheeler started a law practice in Nacogdoches. He was appointed district attorney and then district judge. Wheeler became a justice of the State Supreme Court in 1845. He became chief justice in 1857 and he was still serving in that office when he killed himself in 1864.

1

2

3

1) The famous Route 66 comes right through downtown Shamrock. But most traffic now moves on Interstate 40. Travelers on the new route barely get a glimpse of Shamrock. Motels, garages and eating places built on the old route in the 1950s are now vacant. Far more vehicles are on the highways today and far fewer roadside garages are operating. Some people still claim the old cars were better than today's cars, despite this evidence to the contrary.
2) Green shamrocks are embossed on the sidewalks of Shamrock. The big event is St. Patrick's Day, of course.
3) The Pioneer West Museum in an old hotel building at 206 North Madden in Shamrock is open weekdays and Sunday afternoons. There is no fee.

HEMPHILL COUNTY

Ranald Mackenzie is the U.S. Army officer most often credited with clearing the Comanches off these Plains. The troops he brought up from the frontier forts to the south accomplished the final humiliation of Chief Quanah Parker. But the Comanche War was more than just a contest between Mackenzie and Quanah Parker. The army also sent troops into the Comanches' Panhandle hunting grounds from Fort Sill

1

2

1) Frontier scout Billy Dixon and five other men stood off an Indian war party here for three days in September of 1874. Dixon was working for General Nelson Miles when this Buffalo Wallow Fight occurred. The general got him a Medal of Honor for his performance.

2) A standard metal historical marker on State Highway 33 southeast of Canadian recalls how Captain Wyllys Lyman and 95 troopers stood off 400 Indians in September of 1874. This marker is at the actual site, about four miles off the highway.

3) The present Hemphill County Courthouse in Canadian was built in 1909.

3

in the Oklahoma Territory and from Fort Leavenworth in Kansas.

There was some action here in what is now Hemphill County between the Indians and the forces commanded by General Nelson Miles from Fort Leavenworth. Miles had a headquarters camp for a while in 1874 on the bank of the Washita River. One of his supply trains was ambushed by Comanches and Kiowas northeast of the base camp on September 9 and a small party of four soldiers and two civilian scouts was attacked a few miles southeast of the camp on September 12. Miles' men were vastly outnumbered in both engagements but they stood off the Indians and survived.

The Canadian River crosses northern Hemphill County so there was traffic through here long before the first Spaniards came. Traces of Pueblan settlements dating to 1200 A.D. have been found in several places along the valley of the Canadian. But valley is not the word usually used here. People in the Panhandle use the term ''Breaks of the Canadian'' in referring to the broken and eroded landscape along the river and its big network of tributaries. The name Canadian probably comes from the Spanish word ''canada.'' It means

1   2

1) *The Hemphill County Library occupies a handsome building the Women's Christian Temperance Union built in 1911 at Main and 5th, across the street from the courthouse.*
2) *The first public building built in Hemphill County was the jail. It has been standing here on the courthouse square since 1890.*
3) *The old Moody Hotel was built in 1910. There was a county museum in this building until it was remodeled into an office building in the 1970s. There is a coffee shop now in the space the museum occupied.*

3

"boxed canyon." The Canadian passes out of Texas here at the eastern edge of Hemphill County and joins the Arkansas in Oklahoma.

The principal town in Hemphill County is Canadian, on the river. There had been a little settlement before. It became a town when the Panhandle and Santa Fe Railroad built a line across the river at this point. That was in 1887. The county government was organized the same year and Canadian was designated the county seat. The county had been created with

1

2

1) The skeleton of the old iron bridge was left in place when the new concrete bridge was built on U.S. 83 across the Canadian River.
2) The U.S. Forest Service maintains a small park on Lake Marvin east of Canadian. There is a fee for camping and fishing.
3) The end of price controls brought the oil scouts and drillers back to Hemphill County and most of the other counties on the Plains.
4) The late railroad magnate Robert R. Young was born in Canadian in 1897. Young pioneered lightweight passenger trains in the early 1940s as chairman of the Chesapeake and Ohio. He later headed the New York Central.

3

4

most of the other counties in this part of the state in 1876. The legislature named it for John Hemphill. He came to Texas from South Carolina in 1838 and took up the practice of law. He served on the Supreme Court of the Republic and he was the first chief justice of the State Supreme Court after annexation. Hemphill was representing Texas in the U.S. Senate when the state seceded in 1861. He was serving in the Congress of the Confederacy when he died in Virginia in 1862.

There is some farming in Hemphill County but livestock is a bigger factor in the economy than farming. Oil was discovered here in 1955 and the income from the oil and gas wells is ten times what the farms and ranches here earn.

The Lipscomb County government is about the only thing happening in the little town of Lipscomb. The dignified courthouse was built in 1916 but the windows and doors have been changed.

LIPSCOMB COUNTY

This is the northeast corner of the Texas Panhandle. Lipscomb County is bounded by western Oklahoma on the east and by the Oklahoma Panhandle on the north. The main business is ranching. Wheat is the main crop. Oil and gas earn most of the income. The oil was discovered in 1956. There are no large towns. The population of Lipscomb County is under 4,000. The biggest town has fewer than 1,000 people. The county seat has fewer than 200.

Lipscomb County was created by the legislature in 1876. There were a few settlers on Wolf Creek in the center of the county by 1880. This settlement became the town of Lipscomb and it was designated the county seat when the county government was organized in 1887. Lipscomb never got rail service. Several other towns in the county did and four other towns in Lipscomb County are bigger than Lipscomb. But the county government remains in Lipscomb.

The biggest town in Lipscomb County moved here from Oklahoma. Booker was established at the northwest corner of the county as a shipping point when the Panhandle and Santa Fe Railroad built a line across the northern end of the county in 1917. The people living in a little town called La Kemp, on the other side of the Oklahoma line, closed up their town and moved to Booker to be on the railroad. The same rail line put the towns of Darrouzett and Follett on the map. Higgins is the oldest railroad town in the county. It developed around a shipping point and water tank the Panhandle and Santa Fe established in 1886 when it was laying tracks from the Oklahoma border to Canadian. Higgins, Follett, Darrouzett and Booker all were named for railroad officials.

Lipscomb and Lipscomb County were named for Abner S. Lipscomb. He had been a lawyer and a member of the legislature and a supreme court justice in his home state of South Carolina before he moved to Texas in 1838. He did not exactly start his Texas career on the bottom rung. President

1) One of the most popular entertainers of the 1920s and 1930s spent some time here in Lipscomb County before he became famous. Will Rogers became a star of network radio and movies before he was killed in a plane crash in 1935. But he started on the stage, drawling jokes while he performed fancy tricks with a lariat. Will was born in Oklahoma. He perfected some of his rope tricks while he was working as a cowboy on the Ewing ranch outside Higgins.
2) Downtown Higgins looked like this when Rogers was a young cowboy.

Lamar made him secretary of state in 1839. Lipscomb was elected to the State Supreme Court after Annexation and he was still serving on the court when he died in Austin in 1856.

Historians believe Coronado came through what is now Lipscomb County in 1541. Coronado's expedition searched New Mexico and west Texas in 1540 and 1541 for some golden cities the Spanish had heard stories about. They found a few very ordinary Indian villages in New Mexico but then they heard a new story about a golden city called Quivira. It was supposed to be farther east. Coronado and his followers were camped in the Palo Duro Canyon in the summer of 1541 when Coronado decided to send the bulk of his party back to the Rio Grande while he and three dozen horsemen tried to find Quivira. They found it but it was just another Indian town with no gold so they returned to the Rio Grande, too, and eventually to Mexico City.

Will Rogers came to Higgins on a passenger train and he left the same way. Higgins has not seen a passenger train in many years. But the freight trains still run through here. Higgins has not grown very much since Rogers was here.

Four or five Franciscan missionaries traveling with Coronado decided to stay behind to try to convert the Indians. Ungrateful Indians murdered one of the Franciscans in 1544. It is uncertain where Juan de Padilla was killed and buried. But it may have been near Higgins in southeast Lipscomb County. Quivira is believed to have been somewhere near the eastern edge of the Llano Estacado, between here and Kansas. A monument in Ellwood Park in Amarillo describes the Franciscan Juan de Padilla of Andalucia as the first Christian martyr in Texas.

OCHILTREE COUNTY

This is another area thought to have been visited by the earliest Spanish explorers and there was some traffic through here in the 1870s before the first settlers came. The Jones and Plummer Trail came this way. Jones and Plummer were a couple of freighters. They ran regular wagon trains between Dodge City and the buffalo hunters' camp at Mobeetie in Wheeler County. A branch of their wagon road ran through Ochiltree County to Tascosa in Oldham County. There was a trading post on the trail about 13 miles south of the present city of Perryton in 1874.

The legislature created this county in 1876 and named it for William B. Ochiltree. He was born in North Carolina and he practiced law in Alabama before he came to Texas in 1839. Ochiltree was a district judge in East Texas and a member of the legislature before the Civil War. He was a member of the Secession Convention and he raised a regiment for the Confederacy.

There was no settlement in Ochiltree County until after 1880. The Bar C Ranch occupied a big part of the area by

1

2

1) This is probably the oldest house in Perryton. It was built originally in another town. Mrs. John Blasingame built the house in Ochiltree in 1912. Everybody left Ochiltree and moved to Perryton when the government moved in 1919. It was the usual reason. The railroad missed Ochiltree and built a station at Perryton. Ochiltree died.
2) The present Ochiltree County Courthouse was built in Perryton in 1928. Perryton is a busy, prosperous, clean and attractive town of about 8,000.
3) The old Santa Fe depot in Perrytown is being turned into a museum. It is on North Main, about half a mile north of downtown.

3

1885. One of the first settlements was established that year. A party of German immigrants started a town in the west end of the county and called it Wawaka. The town moved three miles in 1919 to get on the railroad line the Panhandle and Santa Fe extended through the county that year. The name of the town was shortened when it moved and it has been Waka ever since. Farnsworth, Perryton, Twitchell and Huntoon all got their starts as stops on the Panhandle and Santa Fe. Farnsworth, Twitchell and Huntoon all were named for officials of the railroad.

Perryton was named for County Judge George Perry. The county government moved to Perryton when the railroad

1

2

3

1) *Some visitors are surprised at the number of lakes in the Panhandle. A dam on Wolf Creek created this one. It is called Lake Fryer.*

2) *Ochiltree County is one of the places where the Panhandle Pueblo Indians lived before Columbus. They had a city here near Lake Fryer about 18 miles southeast of Perryton. Archaeologists found interesting things here in 1919 and 1920. They apparently took all of them away. There is nothing here now but the marker. It is on private property and not easy to find.*

3) *The Jones Trading Post was on what is now Lake Fryer Road, between the lake and U.S. 83.*

came through. A town named Ochiltree had been designated the county seat when the county government was first organized in 1889. But the railroad missed Ochiltree by 15 miles. All the businesses and most of the population followed the government to the new town of Perryton. Some of the buildings were moved. No county seat in Texas is farther north than Perryton. It is just seven miles from the Oklahoma line. It is closer to five other state capitals than it is to Austin.

Much of Ochiltree County is still in ranches and there are some major feedlots here. Income from livestock is greater than from farming. The big farm crops are wheat and feed grains. Oil was discovered in 1951 and there is very substantial production.

ROBERTS COUNTY

Roberts County has a population of about 1,100 and more than 550 wells producing oil and gas worth more than 100 million dollars a year. Sixty-nine other counties produce more oil and gas. But petroleum is the biggest factor in the economy of Roberts County by far. There is some farming and more ranching here, but the income from the livestock

There is some farming in Roberts County and a little irrigation. Most of the population is concentrated in the southeast corner of the county. Most of the rest of the county is in large ranches as it has been since the Indians left. Irrigated land here is worth $600 to $800 an acre; range land about $200.

and crops together is less than the royalty payments from the oil and gas.

Most of the county is in the rugged, broken valley of the Canadian. Most of the population is concentrated in the southeast corner along the railroad the Santa Fe built in 1887.

Roberts County was created in 1876 and named for Oran M. Roberts and John S. Roberts. The two men were not related. They just had the same last name and the legislature wanted to honor both of them. John Roberts came to Texas from Louisiana in the 1820s. He served in the Texas Army during some of the early skirmishing around San Antonio in 1835 and he signed the Declaration of Independence in 1836. He died in 1871. Oran Roberts came to Texas from South Carolina in 1841. He was a lawyer and he became district attorney at San Augustine almost as soon as he settled there. He went on to serve as a district judge and justice of the Supreme Court. He was president of the Secession Convention and a colonel in the Confederate Army. He was serving as chief justice of the State Supreme Court when this county was created and he was later elected governor. Oran Roberts taught law at the University of Texas and wrote several historical works before he died in 1898.

A man named Bill Anderson was the only person living here when Roberts County was created. W.H. Criswell established the first ranch about 1877 or 1878. The building of the railroad in 1887 brought in more settlers. A railroad construction camp in the valley of Red Deer Creek developed into a little town. The settlers gave it the name Miami. The name is said to mean "Sweetheart" in some Indian dialect.

Residents of Miami got up a petition to get a county government organized so they could make their town the

FOSSIL BEDS
(THREE MILES SOUTHEAST)

CITED AS ONE OF MOST PROLIFIC FOSSIL FIELDS OF LOWER PLIOCENE AGE AT TIME OF DISCOVERY, THESE BEDS ARE ABOUT 13,000,000 YEARS OLD. GEOLOGISTS OF RIO BRAVO OIL COMPANY FOUND THEM IN 1928 ON C.C. COFFEE RANCH, AND THEIR REPORTS BROUGHT SPECIALISTS FROM SEVERAL MAJOR INSTITUTIONS TO THE AREA.

THE FOSSIL BONES BURIED HERE INCLUDED (AMONG OTHERS) THOSE OF A PREHISTORIC CAMEL, A KIND OF ANTELOPE, HORSE, BONE-CRUSHING DOG, MASTODON, AND WILD PIG.

FURTHER STUDIES LED SCIENTISTS IN 1941 TO ADOPT "HEMPHILLIAN" AS THE NAME FOR THE GEOLOGIC AGE REPRESENTED BY THESE FOSSILS.
(1970)

1

2

1 & 2) Some of the fossil bones found here near U.S. 60 east of Miami are now in the Roberts County Museum in Miami.

county seat. But there was another contender. People living at a settlement called Oran near the Canadian River wanted the government in their town. There were some gross irregularities when the election was held in January of 1889. Thirty-eight votes were recorded in the little hamlet of Codman where there were just three people eligible to vote. Codman was close to Miami and a long way from Oran. The Cod-

3

3) The Roberts County government moved to Miami in 1898. The present courthouse was built in 1913. Miami is very pleasantly situated in the valley of Red Deer Creek. The people here pronounce the name of the town my-AMUH.

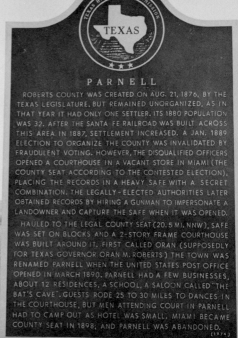

1   2

*1) Roberts County was named for Oran Roberts and John S. Roberts. Oran
Roberts was one of our more durable public officials. He came to Texas from
Alabama in 1841. His first public office was district attorney at San
Augustine in 1844. He was later a judge, a justice of the Supreme Court,
chief justice and governor. Roberts had as much as anyone to do with arrang-
ing the Texas secession in 1861. He was governor when the University of
Texas opened in 1883 and he taught law at the university for ten years after he
left the governor's office. His students at the law school referred to him as
the "Old Alcalde."
2) Only a marker is left at the site of the town that was the original county
seat of Roberts County.*

man votes helped Miami win the contest. But the result was
ruled void because of all the funny business. The leading vote-
getters in the election for county offices impounded the
returns and locked them up in a safe in a store building in
Miami that they declared to be the temporary courthouse.

The people of Oran apparently had the right on their side
and they had a little might, too. They sent a gunman to Miami
to steal the safe. They hauled it to Oran and built a frame
courthouse around it and installed their own set of county officials. They changed the name of their town to Parnell and
Parnell was the county seat until 1898. The voters decided in
another election that year to move the government to Miami.
Miami is still the county seat and the principal town. Three-
quarters of the people in the county live in Miami. Parnell has
disappeared.

Gray County was named for Peter Gray. He was a district attorney, member of the legislature, member of the Confederate Congress, justice of the Texas Supreme Court and deeply interested in Texas history. He financed Henderson Yoakum's **History of Texas.** *His father wrote what probably is the best account of the Convention of 1836 that produced the Texas Declaration of Independence.*

GRAY COUNTY

One of the last engagements in the last big campaign against the Plains Indians occurred here in Gray County. It was a couple of months after Ranald Mackenzie's troops had broken up the main Indian camp in the Palo Duro Canyon and scattered the Kiowas and Cheyennes and Comanches allied with Quanah Parker. Chief Grey Beard and 300 Cheyennes were camped here on McClellan Creek. Lieutenant Frank Baldwin discovered Grey Beard's camp on November 8, 1874. Baldwin was a very experienced lieutenant. He had advanced all the way to lieutenant colonel in the Union Army during the Civil War. He joined the U.S. Army regulars after the war as a lieutenant and he eventually was promoted to major general. But that November afternoon on McClellan Creek he was a lieutenant with a small body of foot soldiers and two dozen empty supply wagons. Baldwin put his soldiers in the wagons and attacked the Indian camp. He ran off the Cheyennes and rescued two white girls the Indians had taken prisoner more than a year earlier. The Indian problem was almost ended. The legislature divided the Panhandle into counties less than two years later and named this county for William Fairfax Gray's son Peter.

William Fairfax Gray was a Virginian and he was working as a land agent when he came to Texas the first time in 1835. He was at the Convention of 1836 as a spectator. He did not stay for the revolution. But he came back again in 1837 with his wife and son and settled in Houston. Peter Gray studied law in his father's office. He succeeded his father as district attorney and he also served as a district judge before the Civil War. Peter was a member of the Confederate Congress during the war and he was with General John Magruder at the battle of Galveston in 1863. He died in 1874.

1

2

1) The courthouse Gray County built in 1928 is not pretentious. But the county is rich. There is substantial industry and the farms and ranches are dotted with oil and gas wells. The streets of Pampa are brick, wide and clean.

2) The old headquarters building of the White Deer Land Company in Pampa is now a museum. The White Deer Company subdivided and developed 600,000 acres of land in Gray and three adjoining counties between 1886 and 1957.

3) There are free campsites and hookups in Hobart Street Park.

3

One of the early settlements in Gray County was on McClellan Creek about 10 miles west of the place where Lieutenant Baldwin and Chief Grey Beard fought. R.P. Reeves and a few other farmers moved in during the early 1880s. The settlement became the town of Alanreed when the Chicago, Rock Island and Gulf Railroad came through. Rancher George Saunders had a headquarters camp near the center of the county. Pierre Lefors started a settlement near the camp sometime before 1900 and his settlement became the town of Lefors. The town was designated the county seat when the county government was organized in 1902. The population of Lefors got up to about 150 by 1910 but it had declined to under 50 by 1928 when the residents of the county voted to move the government to Pampa.

Pampa had been established about 1888 to be a shipping point on the Santa Fe Railroad. The discovery of oil in the county in 1925 made Pampa a very important shipping point and it has become a very pleasant city. Twenty-five thousand people live in Gray County, now, and 20,000 of them live in Pampa. The name comes from the Spanish word "pampas."

1

2

3

1) The Alanreed-McLean Area Museum in Alanreed is open daily except Sunday.

2) The federal government bought scattered tracts of land across the Panhandle and in Oklahoma and New Mexico after the great dust storms of the 1930s. These national grasslands have been allowed to go back to native grass and brush to anchor the soil and help prevent dust storms. There are provisions for picnicking, camping, fishing and boating in the Lake McClellan National Grassland area in southern Gray County. There is a fee.

3) Lake McClellan is near the site where Lieutenant Frank Baldwin rescued Julia and Adelaide Germain from the Cheyennes.

It means plains.

Livestock from the ranches and feedlots outranks crops in economic importance here. Oil and gas outrank agriculture.

CARSON COUNTY

All of the nuclear and thermonuclear bombs for the United States' arsenals are assembled at a plant in the southwest corner of this county. The Pantex plant sprawls over several thousand acres on the line between Carson County and Potter County. Pantex made ordinary bombs during World War II. The plant was converted to super weapons in 1951.

Carson County was created in 1876. The first house was the headquarters of the White Deer Ranch on White Deer Creek. It was built in the early 1880s. Samuel Burk Burnett's 6666 Ranch was running cattle in the area by the middle 1880s. Settlers started filing on state lands when the Panhandle and Santa Fe Railroad came in 1887. The railroad had its terminus for a while at what is now the town of Panhandle. The town was being called Panhandle City at the time. It was designated

1

3

1) *A stone likeness of a white deer stands on a pedestal in the middle of the main intersection in the town of White Deer. The town was named for White Deer Creek.*

2) *Houses co ered with asbestos siding all look alike, but this is said to be the oldest house in Carson County. It is a rent house, now, but it was headquarters for the N-Bar-N Ranch in 1887.*

3) *The barn looks older than the house but it does not appear likely to be here much longer. The N-Bar-N Ranch operated on land leased from The Francklyn Land and Cattle Company. Francklyn was owned by British interests including the Cunard Lines. The company went broke and was reorganized as the White Deer Land Company. White Deer put the N-Bar-N out of business and started subdividing the land. The last great cattle drive to the Montana ranges was organized here in 1892.*

the county seat when the county was organized in 1888. Panhandle is the principal city in the county. White Deer is the second biggest city in the county. It and the White Deer Ranch were named for the creek here where Indians claimed they used to see a white deer.

Carson County was named for Samuel P. Carson. He was born in North Carolina and he held several public offices there before he bought some land on the Red River in 1835. He probably was not a resident of Texas when he was elected to represent the Red River area at the Convention of 1836.

1

2

3

1) *The outstanding Square House Museum in Panhandle is open daily and on Sunday afternoon.*
2) *The Carson County Courthouse was built in Panhandle in 1950.*
3) *Pesticides have killed the tree reputed to be the first in the area.*
4) *The Pantex Plant in western Carson County assembles nuclear and thermonuclear bombs from components manufactured elsewhere.*

4

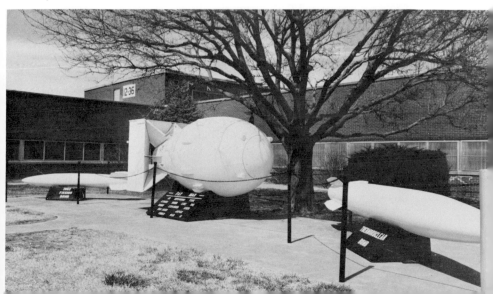

Yankee traders ran wagon trains between Missouri and Arkansas and the Mexican town of Santa Fe from the 1820s until the 1880s. One branch of the Santa Fe Trail crossed the Texas Panhandle and came through what is now Carson County. The trail marker here on State Highway 136 is new. Vandals stole the previous marker.

The convention had already adopted the Declaration of Independence when Carson reached Washington-on-the-Brazos, but he signed his name to the document when he did arrive, on March 10. The convention named Carson secretary of state in the interim government and then sent him to the United States to gather up men, money and supplies for the revolution. Carson spent a good bit of his own money on the cause. Having this county named for him 38 years after he died was his reward.

There has been substantial production of oil and gas here since the first discovery was made in 1921. The county has more than 100,000 acres of farmland under irrigation. The principal crops are grains. They earn more money than the livestock in this county.

HUTCHINSON COUNTY

Two major battles between Indians and whites were fought around an abandoned trading post in this county. The post was built by William Bent in the late 1830s or early 1840s. This was before the Texans and the Plains Indians had concluded that Texas was not big enough for Texans and Plains Indians, too. But Bent's venture was a risky one and he knew it. He built a sturdy adobe building like a fort on one of the little creeks feeding into the Canadian River. It had no windows, just one door and gun ports. It was fairly safe. But the Indians never really took to the idea of having a trading post so far inside their territory and Bent gave it up after a few years. The fort was abandoned by probably 1845 but it stood for a long time. It was on one of the routes the Indians used regularly. The Comanches and Kiowas sometimes took shelter inside the walls and often camped around the building. It was a major landmark in the Panhandle. It was labelled Adobe Walls on all the maps of the day.

1   2

1) The Hutchinson County Museum in Borger features exhibits dealing with the county's oil boom. The boom years here were the late 1920s. The population then was about three times what it is today.
2) The U.S. Bureau of Reclamation built Lake Meredith on the Canadian in the 1960s. This is a large lake, extending into Moore and Potter counties. The National Park Service maintains several parks around the shores. Visitors can camp up to ten days. There are no hookups but there are no fees, either.

The Comanches and the Kiowas took sides during the Civil War. Some of them signed treaties with the Confederates and some signed with the Union. Some of them changed sides more than once. Most whites regarded most Plains Indians as enemies most of the time. They were always more reliable as enemies. A big band of Comanches and Kiowas smashed a Confederate outpost in Young County in October of 1864.

3) It looks more like a high school in Dallas, but this is the Hutchinson County Courthouse in Stinnett. It was completed in 1928, during the oil boom.

3

Two major engagements between whites and Indians occurred near the ruined trading post known as Adobe Walls in what is now Hutchinson County. Granite monuments mark the site on the Turkey Track Ranch. The battleground is in northeast Hutchinson County and accessible from Farm Road 281.

But just two months later a Union force was invading what is now Hutchinson County under orders to find and attack the Comanche and Kiowa winter camps. The Union troops were cavalrymen from New Mexico commanded by Colonel Christopher "Kit" Carson. There were about 400 of them. They surprised a band of Kiowas in their camp near the adobe ruin but a few of the Kiowas got away and aroused the Comanches in their big camp nearby. It was like Carson had kicked an anthill. There were Indians everywhere. The troops ducked into the abandoned fort and fought from there all day. They sensibly withdrew after dark and Carson later reported to his superiors that it would require 1,000 men to take and hold Adobe Walls. The number of Indians there that November day was estimated between 3,000 and 7,000. Carson was credited with a victory in getting his troops out of the place.

The white buffalo hunters were in this part of the Panhandle by 1872, and Adobe Walls was one of the places they established a camp. Several traders and a blacksmith set up shops in the camp and a number of hunters made the camp their headquarters. The Plains Indians were beside themselves over the slaughter of the buffalo. It was clear to them that once the buffalo were gone the only life available to Indians would be on the hated reservations. A buffalo hunters' camp was an affront and a threat that had to be dealt with.

Several hundred Comanches, Cheyennes and Kiowas led by Quanah Parker and Lone Wolf attacked the camp of Adobe Walls on June 27, 1874. There were 28 men and one woman in the camp. One of their tents had collapsed. They were awake and working on that so they were not taken completely

1   2

1) The first battle of Adobe Walls has to be counted a draw but the Indians were the clear losers in the second battle. One woman and 28 men stood off hundreds of Indians. Most of the whites were buffalo hunters armed with high powered rifles. One of them was Billy Dixon and his marksmanship was one of the factors that demoralized the Indians. One of Dixon's shots knocked a Cheyenne brave off his horse at a distance of almost a mile. The Indians took it as a bad omen. This same Billy Dixon was the hero of the Buffalo Wallow Fight. He was later the first sheriff of Hutchinson County and he had a home for a time at the site of the Adobe Walls battle. This granite marker lists the names of all the whites present at the second battle of Adobe Walls.
2) A similar monument nearby lists the names of the Comanche and Cheyenne leaders killed in the same battle.

off guard when the Indians swarmed onto the scene at dawn. Four of the hunters were killed in the first few hours of fighting. The others kept up a steady fire with their powerful rifles. The Indians milled around the camp for several days and then drifted away as more hunters showed up to reinforce those in the camp. This was just three months before Colonel Mackenzie retired Quanah Parker at Palo Duro. Some people believed that the Indians might have gained enough momentum to hold out a few more years if they had won this second battle of Adobe Walls.

All the fighting at Adobe Walls happened before the legislature created Hutchinson County in 1876. The buffalo were about gone by then. The hunters were leaving. The cattlemen came next. There were just 15 families in the county in 1889. One of the first settlements was Plemmons but Stinnett was designated the county seat when the county government was organized in 1901. Stinnett was named for A.S. Stinnett of Amarillo.

Stinnett was the principal city in the county until A.P. Borger laid out the city of Borger during the oil boom in 1926.

Bat Masterson was the individual at Adobe Walls with the name most familiar to most people today. Bat had been hunting buffalo on the Plains for a couple of years before he got caught up in the fight here. He later was sheriff at Dodge City and it was there he did most of the things that later attracted the attention of TV and movie writers. Bat was working for a newspaper in New York when he died in 1921.

The oil and Borger's exuberant advertising lured 45,000 people to Borger in the first year. The population is only about 15,000 now, but Borger is still the biggest city in the county with several plants serving the oil and petrochemical industry. The first oil strike in Hutchinson County was in 1923. The oil and gas wells earn more than 100 million dollars a year and this is about five times what the crops and livestock bring in.

The northwest corner of the county is high plain. Most of the rest of the county is in the valley of the Canadian. Evidence of an Indian pueblo from about 1200 A.D. has been found on Antelope Creek near Fritch. The site is listed in *The National Register of Historic Places.*

Hutchinson County was named for Anderson Hutchinson. He was born in Virginia and he practiced law in Tennessee, Alabama and Mississippi before he came to Texas and opened a law office in Austin, in 1840. Hutchinson was appointed district judge in 1841. He was holding court in San Antonio when Mexican General Adrian Woll raided the town in 1842. Woll took the judge and all the lawyers, witnesses and jurors into custody and marched them to Mexico City. The judge was locked up in Perote Prison until the U.S. Ambassador managed to get him released in 1843. He promptly resigned his Texas office and moved back to Mississippi.

HANSFORD COUNTY

One of the white hunters drawn to the Texas Plains by the great buffalo slaughter of the 1870s settled down here and became a prominent citizen and public official. James H. Cator was born in Ireland in 1851. He came to the United States when he was 20. James was 21 and in Dodge City when

Windmills almost disappeared from the Plains a few years ago when electricity and fuel for pump engines were cheap. J. B. Buchanan grew up on the Plains and windmills were a part of the scene he did not want to part with. So Buchanan started collecting and restoring old windmills in the 1960s. He has ten different models set up and operating behind the house on his farm south of Spearman. Buchanan is in his 70s and still working on windmills. He advises the Smithsonian on the subject and the Eclipse windmill on display at the Smithsonian was donated by J. B. Buchanan.

the word reached there in 1872 that leather tanneries were willing to pay good prices for buffalo hides. James Cator joined the buffalo hunters and his brother Bob joined him. They had a hunting camp on North Palo Duro Creek for about three years. The Cators converted their place into a trading post in 1875. It was on the wagon road between Dodge City and Tascosa. Cator's Zulu Stockade became a regular stop for the wagon trains and stagecoaches.

James Cator decided he had found a home. Two more brothers and a sister came to join James and Bob on the frontier. They were the first permanent settlers in what the legislature by 1876 had designated as Hansford County. The Cators started ranching about 1878. More settlers began arriving in Hansford County in the 1880s. There were two settlements by the time the county government was organized in

1

2

3

1) The Hansford County Courthouse was built in Spearman in 1931. The original county seat was Hansford. The government moved to Spearman in 1928.

2) There is a small museum at 502 South Davis Street in Spearman. It is in the cottage the Santa Fe built for the railroad stationmaster when the railroad arrived in 1920. The museum is open Tuesdays through Saturdays. There is no fee but donations are encouraged.

3) The Spearman Hotel is older than the town of Spearman. It was built originally in Hansford and moved here when the railroad came. Several shops occupy the building now.

1889. The settlements of Farwell and Hansford contended for the county seat. Hansford won and Farwell disappeared. James Cator was elected county judge and he later became the first banker in the county. One of his brothers was the first sheriff.

Hansford was the county seat and principal town in the county until the early 1920s. The North Texas and Santa Fe Railroad built a line across the southeast corner of the county in 1920. The line missed Hansford by six miles. Businesses began moving from Hansford south to the new town of Spearman on the railroad. Residents of the county voted in 1928 to move the county government to Spearman. It is now the principal town in the county. Hansford has not disappeared entirely. There is a cemetery and there are a few houses still, but it is no longer a town.

Spearman was named for a railroad man, of course. Hansford and Hansford County were named for Dr. John M. Hansford. He apparently had some legal training as well as medical training before he moved from Kentucky to Texas in 1837. Anyway, he was appointed a district judge after he had served two terms in the Congress of the Republic. Hansford somehow got entangled in the feud between the Regulators

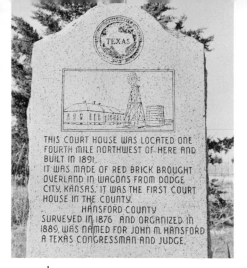

THIS COURT HOUSE WAS LOCATED ONE FOURTH MILE NORTHWEST OF HERE AND BUILT IN 1891.
IT WAS MADE OF RED BRICK BROUGHT OVERLAND IN WAGONS FROM DODGE CITY, KANSAS. IT WAS THE FIRST COURT HOUSE IN THE COUNTY.
HANSFORD COUNTY SURVEYED IN 1876 AND ORGANIZED IN 1889, WAS NAMED FOR JOHN M. HANSFORD A TEXAS CONGRESSMAN AND JUDGE.

1

1) The original courthouse at Hansford was torn down when the government moved to Spearman. The bricks were used to build a church that has since burned.

2

2) Most of the buffalo hunters went on to other pursuits after the buffalo were all killed. The Cators stayed and opened a trading post near this spot on the present State Highway 136 south of Gruver. The Cators were English. They invited two more brothers and a sister to come join them here when they decided to stay. Miss Cator was the only white woman in the county for the first year or so. She probably could have testified to the accuracy of the old saying about Texas being Heaven for men and dogs and hell for women and oxen. The Cators became leading citizens and prominent businessmen. James and Bob are buried in Hansford Cemetery.

and the Moderators in Shelby County in the early 1840s. The Regulators killed him in 1844.

Hansford County produces some oil and a lot of gas. The first discovery was made in 1937. There are some big feedlots in this county and the income from the livestock and farm crops about equals that from the oil and gas wells. Feed grains and wheat are the principal farm crops. About 200,000 acres are irrigated.

SHERMAN COUNTY

This county at the northern edge of the Panhandle is another place where a buffalo hunter was the first permanent settler. J.D. Rawlings settled on Coldwater Creek in the 1870s and started ranching when the buffalo were all gone. W.B. Slaughter bought the Rawlings ranch and a cowboy camp on

1

1) *The Sherman County government moved from Coldwater to Stratford in 1901. The present courthouse in Stratford was built in 1928.*
2) *This county is named for General Sidney Sherman. He fought the Mexicans at San Jacinto and he was commandant of Galveston briefly during the Civil War.*
3) *The small Sherman House Museum and Gallery at 212 North Main in Stratford is free but it is open only by appointment.*

2   3

the Slaughter place was designated the county seat when the county government was organized in 1889. The camp on the creek became the town of Coldwater. It had the only post office in the county and a population of 34 in 1890. The first Sherman County courthouse was built in Coldwater in 1891. There was little increase in the population until 1900. The Chicago, Rock Island and Gulf Railroad built a line across the northwest corner of the county that year. The rail line attracted settlers and they did not settle at Coldwater. The county seat was several miles from the railroad. The

This is the only building still standing where the town of Coldwater was. It was the main unit in the Coldwater wagon yard. The wagon yards were the frontier equivalents of motels. Most towns had some kind of hotel, too, but they all had wagon yards and travelers often stayed in them with their teams and wagons overnight.

newcomers settled at Stratford.

An Englishman named Walter Colton had started the settlement at Stratford in 1885, a few miles up Coldwater Creek from Coldwater. Nothing here remotely resembles anything in the town that Shakespeare knew. But it is said that Colton named his settlement for Stratford-upon-Avon. The railroad drew the population and business to Stratford. The government followed.

There were hard feelings in Coldwater after the voters decided in 1901 to move the county seat to Stratford. Armed volunteers kept watch over the tent in Stratford where the county records were kept until the new courthouse was built. *The Handbook of Texas* says the first court business in Stratford was the return of an indictment against William Bonney. It must have been just a formality. Bonney was the notorious "Billy the Kid." He had led a gang of cattle thieves in the Panhandle in 1879 and he probably did whatever it was the Stratford indictment alleged. But Billy had been dead for 20 years when the indictment was returned. Pat Garrett shot him to death in New Mexico in 1881.

More than half the small population of Sherman County lives in Stratford today. The only other town is Texhoma. It is also on the Rock Island line and it straddles the state line. The banks and the post office and part of the business district of Texhoma are in Oklahoma.

Agriculture and petroleum are about equally important in the economy here. Gas and oil wells earn more than 75

REMOVAL OF ARCHIVES FROM
COLDWATER TO STRATFORD

ON MAY 2, 1901, AN ELECTION WAS HELD TO DETERMINE
WHETHER THE SHERMAN COUNTY SEAT SHOULD BE MOVED
FROM COLDWATER (A RANCHING CENTER IN THE CENTRAL
PART OF THE COUNTY) TO STRATFORD (A GROWING TOWN ON
THE NEW RAILROAD). PARTISAN FEELINGS RAN HIGH AND
THE LEGALITY OF CERTAIN VOTES WAS QUESTIONED.

BECAUSE OF A THREATENED INJUNCTION AGAINST THE
MOVE, A SPECIAL SESSION OF COURT WAS HELD AT 1 A.M.
ON MAY 6. VOTES WERE CANVASSED AND, UNDER COVER OF
DARKNESS, THE COUNTY RECORDS WERE SPIRITED TO A TENT
ABOUT 2 BLOCKS SOUTH OF HERE. A HORSEMAN BRINGING
THE INJUNCTION TO HALT THE MOVE ARRIVED TOO LATE.
FOR SEVERAL DAYS APPREHENSIVE STRATFORD CITIZENS
KEPT AN ARMED GUARD POSTED AROUND THE TENT.

PROPONENTS OF COLDWATER THEN FILED A SUIT TITLED
"W. B. SLAUGHTER ET AL. VS. D. W. SNYDER ET AL.", BUT BY
THE TIME COURT CONVENED, STRATFORD HAD BEEN WIDELY
ACCEPTED AS COUNTY SEAT AND THE SUIT WAS DISMISSED.

THOSE WHO HELPED MOVE THE RECORDS INCLUDED D.W.
SNYDER, COUNTY JUDGE; C. F. RUDOLPH, COUNTY CLERK;
DICK PINCHAM, SHERIFF; D. D. SPURLOCK, DEPUTY SHERIFF;
TOM CHAMBERS, TREASURER; W. J. POTTS AND J.H. BOWMAN,
JR. COMMISSIONERS; AND J. M. UPSHAW, A HIRED FREIGHTER.
(1969)

1) There was no real violence, as there was in some similar contests elsewhere in Texas but the residents of Coldwater exhibited considerable reluctance to give up the county seat after they lost the election in 1901. It was another case of the railroad making the difference. Stratford had rail service and Coldwater did not. This marker is on the courthouse at Stratford.
3) The boundary line between Texas and Oklahoma runs right through Texhoma. Oklahoma is on the left, Texas on the right.

1

2

million dollars a year. The livestock and crops earn almost as much. There are some large feedlots and more than 200,000 acres under irrigation.

Sherman County was named for General Sidney Sherman. He was one of the heroes of the Texas Revolution. Sidney Sherman was born in Massachusetts in 1805 and he died in Galveston in 1873. He worked in Boston and New York and Cincinnati before he acquired his own business in Kentucky in 1831. Sherman was manufacturing cotton bagging and sheet lead when he got interested in Texas in 1835. He sold his business and used part of the money to recruit and equip 52 volunteers to fight the Mexicans in Texas. The flag he and his volunteers brought here with them was the only flag the Tex-

Louis Dumas bought the land where Dumas is today and he laid out the town. Dumas' town was designated the county seat when Moore County was organized the same year, just as he intended. But Louis Dumas was discouraged by a severe winter in 1895. He moved back to Grayson County. He never returned, but the county seat still carries his name. Louis was the son of James Dumas. James surveyed downtown Dallas for John Neely Bryan. He never expected much of Dallas and did not claim the city lots Bryan offered him for his fee.

ans carried at the battle of San Jacinto. Sherman commanded the Texas Army's left wing at San Jacinto as a lieutenant colonel. He was elected a major general of the militia after the government of the republic was organized. One of his duties in that office was to preside over the court-martial of the man Moore County was named for. Moore County adjoins Sherman County on the south.

MOORE COUNTY

This county was named for the commanding officer of the second Texas Navy. The ships assembled for the original navy during the revolution were all destroyed or lost by 1837. The government of the republic started putting the second fleet together in the fall of 1838. The government bought a second-hand steamer and ordered six new schooners, sloops and brigs from a yard in Baltimore. President Lamar picked a young officer of the United States Navy to be the commander of this fleet. Edwin W. Moore was trained at Annapolis but he was only a lieutenant and just 29 years old when Lamar put him in charge of the Texas Navy in 1839. He got a lot of experience in a short time but it was not all naval experience.

President Lamar rented the fleet to the Mexican state of Yucatan just before he left office. Yucatan was rebelling against the Mexican central government and willing to pay 8,000 dollars a month for the navy. Sam Houston succeeded Lamar and immediately cancelled the deal with Yucatan. But the fleet had already sailed. Houston's orders did not reach Commodore Moore until March of 1842. He returned to Galveston in May. The crew of the schooner *San Antonio* mutinied while the ship was in a repair yard in New Orleans.

1

2

1) Dumas is the only county seat Moore County has ever had. The present courthouse was built in 1931 about the time the effects of the Crash of '29 were reaching Texas.

2) There are several exhibits in the Moore County Historical Museum depicting life here in the 1890s and early 1900s. The address is Dumas Avenue and 8th. The museum is open weekdays except Mondays and on Sunday afternoons. There is no fee for admission.

3) One of the earliest fences in the Panhandle was built jointly by the Canadian River ranchers and it extended through Moore County. The fence was to keep northern cows from drifting down into the breaks of the Canadian. The old wagon road between Dodge City and Tascosa came through Moore County, too, close to the present city of Dumas. Dumas today is a prosperous city with some industry and a lot of oil and gas, surrounded by a rich agricultural area.

TEXAS

SITE OF
HISTORIC DRIFT FENCE

UNTIL THE MID-1890'S, NO RANGE FENCES EXISTED IN THE TEXAS PANHANDLE. THUS WHEN WINTER BLIZZARDS CAME, CATTLE DRIFTED FROM OKLAHOMA, COLORADO AND KANSAS TO THE TEXAS RANCHES OF [T] ("BOXT"—DOMINION CATTLE CO., LTD.), K ("SEVEN K"—YORK, PARKER & DRAPER), CC ("BAR C's"—CRESWELL LAND & CATTLE CO.), ("TURKEY TRACK"—HANSFORD LAND & CATTLE CO.), LX (BATES & BEALS) LIT (LITTLEFIELD) AND LE (LEE & REYNOLDS). THE INFLUX CAUSED THESE RANCHES IN THE CANADIAN RIVER BREAKS TO BE OVERGRAZED, FOR BY SPRING ROUNDUP THERE WERE AS MANY NORTHERN AS LOCAL CATTLE IN THE HERDS.

TO PREVENT THE COSTLY AND TIME-CONSUMING JOB OF SEPARATING THE CATTLE, EACH TEXAS RANCHER AGREED TO CONSTRUCT A FENCE ALONG HIS NORTH BOUNDARY LINE. THE RESULTING FENCE WAS 200 MILES LONG AND RAN FROM THE NORTHEAST CORNER OF THE PANHANDLE SOUTHWEST TO NEAR THE SITE WHERE DUMAS WAS LATER FOUNDED, THEN WEST ABOUT 35 MILES INTO NEW MEXICO. IT WAS A 4-STRAND, 4-BARB FENCE WITH POSTS 30 FEET APART AND A GATE EVERY 3 MILES. THE MATERIALS AMOUNTED TO ABOUT 65 CARLOADS OF WIRE AND POSTS HAULED FROM DODGE CITY.

IN 1890, HOWEVER, TO COMPLY WITH AN 1889 STATE LAW PROHIBITING ANY FENCE FROM CROSSING OR ENCLOSING PUBLIC PROPERTY, MOST OF THE FENCE WAS REMOVED.

3

The *San Antonio* later disappeared during a cruise in the Gulf. Little else happened until 1844 when Commodore Moore took the fleet to New Orleans for repairs. Sam Houston was economizing and he held up the appropriations. Moore had to pay the shipyard several thousand dollars of his own money. Houston wanted the fleet returned to Texas and he sent three commissioners to New Orleans to impress this upon the commodore. The commodore was afraid the president wanted to sell the fleet. Moore was back in touch with the rebels in Yucatan by this time. They wanted his help and he wanted to go help them. He talked Houston's commissioners into letting him go and one of them went with him. The Texas fleet clashed with Mexican ships three times during April and May off the coast of Yucatan. President Houston was so upset that he disowned the fleet. He accused Moore of piracy and he appealed to any friendly nation to seize the

1

2

1) Lake Meredith extends across the southeastern corner of Moore County. This is the biggest lake in the Panhandle. It covers more than 21,000 acres. It was built by the U.S. Bureau of Reclamation. The National Park Service supervises the recreation areas around the shore. The campsites and boat ramps like this one at the Blue West Recreation Area off Farm Road 1913 are free.

2) One of the federal government's helium plants is west of U.S. 87 at the southern end of the county. Helium is one gas we are not short of. Helium is used now by divers and scientists as well as by blimp operators. But there is an ample supply stored underground here.

Texas ships and send them home. Moore headed for Galveston as soon as he heard this news. Galveston gave him a hero's welcome. Houston gave him a dishonorable discharge.

The president got the congress to authorize him to sell the four surviving ships. They were put up for auction at Galveston. The people of Galveston intervened to prevent anybody from bidding so the ships remained in Galveston until they were annexed to the U.S. Navy after Texas joined the Union. Moore appealed his discharge to the congress and the congress arranged a court-martial. General Sidney Sherman presided and the court decided in August of 1844 that the commodore's conduct was acceptable under the circumstances. He was reinstated but there was nothing for him to do. He tried to collect damages but he never did.

Settlement proceeded very slowly after Moore County was created in 1876. There were just 15 people living in the county when the county government was organized in 1892. Dumas

The buffalo roam this range no more, but the deer and the antelope still play here. There is a brief open season on deer in the fall. Some limited hunting of the antelope is permitted. Hunting licenses are $5.25 for residents. Several arrangements are available for non-residents at higher fees. You can get information about licenses, seasons and bag limits from 1-800-792-1112, toll free.

was designated the county seat. This town was founded in 1891. Founder Louis Dumas designed it to be the county seat. There were just 23 people in Dumas in 1903 and all their supplies were being hauled in by wagon from Amarillo. The Santa Fe Railroad didn't reach Dumas until 1904. The population spurted after oil was discovered in 1926.

The population of Moore County is only about 15,000 today. But not many counties have more resources. The irrigated farms, feed lots and ranches here produce crops and livestock worth 80 million dollars a year. The value of the oil and gas and helium is more than 250 million dollars a year.

Entertainer Phil Harris used to sing a song about being a Ding Dong Daddy from Dumas. This is the Dumas the song is about. Harris made people aware of it but it was written by Phil Baxter of Navarro County because he got a favorable impression when he had to stop overnight here once on a trip to Denver.

The plains where the XIT Ranch was born still look much the way they looked when the ranch was here except for a few highways. This is Farm Road 767 west of Channing in Hartley County. The XIT originally included about half of Hartley County and two-thirds of Dallam County and portions of eight other counties: Oldham, Deaf Smith, Parmer, Castro, Bailey, Lamb, Cochran and Hockley.

HARTLEY AND DALLAM COUNTIES

These two counties claim to be the heart of the XIT country. The grant the state made to the Capitol Syndicate in return for building the state capitol included most of Dallam County and Hartley County and part of eight other counties. This grant the syndicate developed into the XIT Ranch extended from the northern boundary of Dallam County southward about two hundred miles. These two counties obviously were not in the center. But Buffalo Springs in northern Dallam County was the first XIT headquarters. Channing in Hartley County later was general headquarters. The two counties jointly maintain the XIT Museum in Dalhart. The XIT Rodeo and Reunion are held every summer in Dalhart. The city of Dalhart is the county seat of Dallam County but a good part of the city is in Hartley County. Dalhart is one of the things the two counties have in common.

Hartley County is on the New Mexico border directly south of Dallam County. The town of Hartley on the Fort Worth and Denver line was chosen as the county seat when the county government was voted into existence in 1891. Channing was established as general headquarters for the XIT at the same time, a few miles farther south, on the same railroad.

1

1) The XIT was one of the most famous ranches ever to operate in Texas. John V. Farwell ran it for the syndicate that built the Texas Capitol. He established the first headquarters at Buffalo Springs in northern Dallam County. Some of the early XIT buildings are still standing on what is now the property of the Shamburger Ranch. This was the foreman's house at Buffalo Springs.

2) This picture of XIT cowboys at mealtime was made in 1896. The XIT had a strict set of rules. Employees were forbidden to do any drinking or gambling and they couldn't carry weapons on the ranch.

2

1) The Fort Worth and Denver built a railroad across Hartley County and part of the XIT in 1888. The town of Channing developed on the railroad and became the general headquarters of the XIT. Visitors doing business with the ranch stayed at the Rivers Hotel in Channing.

1

2

3

2) The XIT general office was in this house near the railroad tracks in Channing. The ranch built the house in 1909.

3) J. J. Stockard bought the XIT office in 1949 and he has lived in it ever since. The building is laid out exactly like a house except that there is a large vault off the kitchen where ranch officials presumably kept money and records.

The people at Channing arranged an election in 1896 to move the government to their town. The voters decided that year to keep the government at Hartley. But they decided in another election in 1903 to move the county seat to Channing and Channing has been the county seat ever since. The town was named for George Channing Rivers. He was the paymaster for the Fort Worth and Denver when the tracks were being laid here.

Farming now produces more income than livestock in Hartley County. The big crops are feed grains, wheat and sugar beets. Hartley County has a little natural gas. Dallam County has even less. No oil has been discovered yet in either

1

2

1) The first courthouse in Channing was a frame building that had been built originally at Hartley. XIT employees just put wheels under it and pulled it to Channing with their horses. The old courthouse was converted to a hotel when Hartley County built this courthouse in Channing in 1906.

2) The Methodist church in Channing is said to have been the first Texas church built north of the Canadian River. The Farwells of the XIT were among the founding members. The building was built in 1898.

3) The original Hartley County stone jail stands vacant in the former county seat of Hartley. It was built in 1892.

3

county. But there is oil under some of the former XIT property in other counties so the heirs of the XIT owners still have cause to rejoice every month over the happy fate that brought their ancestors to Texas.

Dallam County is the northwest corner of the Texas Panhandle. It is bounded on the north by the Oklahoma Panhandle and on the west by New Mexico. The first town in the county was Texline on the New Mexico border. Texline was established as a stop on the Fort Worth and Denver Railroad in 1888. More than 100 people were living in Texline by the time the county government was organized in 1891 and the town was designated the county seat. The government moved to Dalhart after another election in 1893. There was some open range ranching here before the state granted most of the area to the Capitol Syndicate in 1882. Livestock still is the biggest factor in the economy of Dallam County but

1

1) Texline is as far west as you can go in the Texas Panhandle. U.S. 87 crosses into New Mexico at the western edge of the town.

2) This part of Texas was a sheep range before it was a cattle range. Mexican residents of New Mexico were in the habit of grazing their flocks on the High Plains.

3) The first cattle rancher here had to deal with the Spanish grandee described in the legend on this historical marker on U.S. 54 in western Hartley County.

4) A large part of northern Dallam County is included in the National Grasslands. The western two-thirds of this county was included in the original boundaries of the XIT Ranch.

2

3

4

1

2

1) The present Dallam County Courthouse was built in Dalhart in 1922.
2) A memorial to the XIT Ranch stands on an island between U.S. 87 and U.S. 385 just north of downtown Dalhart. The memorial was put here during the fifth annual XIT Reunion in 1940. It has been rebuilt twice after trucks hit it.
3) The XIT Museum on 5th Street is open weekday afternoons except Sunday and Monday.

3

farming is almost as important. Feed grains and wheat are the chief crops. The county has more than 200,000 acres of farm land under irrigation.

Dallam County was named for James Wilmer Dallam. He came to Texas from Maryland in 1839. He was a lawyer and writer. He died of yellow fever in Matagorda when he was just 29. But by that time he had compiled a digest of the laws of the Republic of Texas and opinions of the Texas Supreme

1) The XIT Reunion and Rodeo has been held in Dalhart every year since 1937.
2) Few XIT men survive but hundreds of young cowboys show up every year to compete in what is billed as the biggest amateur rodeo in the world.

1

2

Court that has been a valuable reference work for lawyers ever since. Hartley County was also named for a lawyer. Oliver Cromwell Hartley came to Galveston from Virginia in 1846. He served in the state legislature and he also published a digest of Texas laws.

The XIT was one of the most famous ranches in history. It had 150,000 cows on its ranges and 150 cowboys on its payroll at the peak of its operation. But the owners of the XIT were not trying to found a ranching dynasty. John and Charles Farwell and their partners were just trying from the outset to get back the money they spent building the state capitol plus some profit. They had to form a syndicate in England to raise the money to pay for livestock, fencing and salaries when they

There are free meals on the rodeo grounds during the XIT Reunion the first weekend in August. The Reunion hosts serve corn on the cob on Thursday evening, watermelon Friday evening and barbecue Saturday evening.

The XIT Reunions are held in Rita Blanca Park on the south side of Dalhart. There is an admission fee for the rodeo and other events held in the arena during the reunions. But there is no charge for admission to the grounds where the meals are served. There are campsites around this small lake in the park and some hookups but never enough to go around during the reunions. The original XIT Reunion was held in Fort Worth in 1936. The former cowboys voted to hold the 1937 meeting in Dalhart and they have been meeting in Dalhart ever since. Only four former XIT men made it to the 1980 meeting and three of those have since died, but many children and grandchildren attend and strangers are welcome, too.

decided to turn their land into a ranch. They paid off the debt with the profits from the ranch and with the proceeds from land sales. The XIT began selling off land in 1901. The entire debt to the English investors was cleared by 1909. The last XIT cow was sold in 1912. The land the ranch still owned then was leased out until 1950. The last of it was sold that year.

The practice of driving cattle from this part of Texas to Dodge City ended about 1885 because of fences and quarantines. But cattle drives continued for many more years. The XIT and other big outfits discovered that their animals would gain more weight if they spent a year or so on northern ranges before they went to market. The Texas ranchers bought or

The King Ranch probably is as famous as the XIT ever was. But the XIT may have been the most famous brand in the history of ranching. Part of the reason is an old story that the brand was designed to signify "Ten in Texas," with the X standing for the Roman numeral ten. This story has been circulated all over the world, but it is only a story. The ranch did extend into ten counties. But J. Evetts Haley says this probably never entered the mind of the brand's originator. Haley says in **The XIT Ranch of Texas** *that Ab Blocker and ranch manager B. H. Campbell were discussing possible brands after Blocker delivered the first herd of cattle to Buffalo Springs. Blocker suggested XIT and Campbell accepted it. Haley says the consideration was that the brand was easy to apply and difficult to change.*

leased ranges in Montana and Wyoming and drove their animals up there when they reached the age of two years. The cows were shipped to Chicago when they were ready for market. The move from the Panhandle to the northern ranges could have been made by rail after 1887 or 1888. But it was cheaper to drive the herds. Twelve to 15 cowhands could handle 2,500 to 3,000 cows. Some of the legends and some of the music of the cow country came from this period. The ballad about Wyoming being the little dogie's new home is one example and another one is an expression people still use when they are moving from one place to another. The cowboys regularly staked their horses close to their bedrolls when they spent the night on the trail. They never knew when something might spook the cattle and cause them to have to go to work. So they were "pulling up stakes" every morning when they started moving again.

Captain Jack Hays and the Texas Rangers probably started the Texas mystique, chasing Comanches on horseback with six-shooters. The cowboys working these ranges and the trail drives fixed the image permanently in the minds of people around the world. Few of those rugged individuals are left. But there never were a great many. Their legend always was out of proportion to their numbers.

Dust

Farmers like to believe they can at least feed themselves if times get really hard. But this isn't always so. A terrible drought coincided with the Great Depression of the 1930s. Thousands of Plains farmers lost everything. Dust covered their abandoned homes and machines. A dust storm in April of 1935 was so severe that some people on the Plains were frightened into thinking it was the end of the world. It is said that Woody Guthrie composed **So Long, It's Been Good To Know You** during this storm. Guthrie was living in Pampa at the time. The dust still blows on the Plains. Crops still fail occasionally. It is not everybody's idea of the Promised Land. But the dust bowl of the 1930s has become a land of plenty.

4

Some Notes on the Evolution of Agriculture on the Plains

1

1) Some of the land on the Plains still is suitable only for what most of it once was used for. Cattle still graze on the ranges where there is no readily accessible underground water. And a few landowners just prefer to use their land for grazing. But there are more cows in the feed lots, now, at any given time, than there are on the range.

2) Here the animals are fattened for market on a diet worked out by nutrition specialists. Most of the lots feed a combination of corn and sorghum and other grains grown on some of the same lands that once were pastures. Raising cattle was the first agricultural enterprise here after the Indians left. It has become a much more efficient and scientific enterprise in the past few years. But the feed lots are a lot less romantic than the ranges and few places smell worse than a feed lot.

2

1) Most Plains farmers power their irrigation pumps with car or truck engines converted to burn natural gas. The underground water is the lifeblood of the Plains but it is a diminishing resource. Farmers can now claim an allowance on their tax returns for depletion of their water reserves. No agency has power to regulate use of the water but there are some voluntary conservation efforts.

1

2

2) The farmers hook up portable pipes to carry the water directly to their fields.

3) Or they use self-propelled sprinkler systems to make artificial rain. There are two or three versions of the sprinkler systems. The first attempts at farming on the Plains were in the creek and river valleys. The first crops were fruits and vegetables. The first big money crop was wheat even before irrigation was well established. Wheat is still a very important crop on the Plains. But much of the land and much of the water are used now to produce livestock feed. Chemical fertilizers and irrigation have almost eliminated crop failures. But crops are sometimes damaged by wind and hail and once in a great while there is too much rain.

3

1) The Panhandle grain fields attract wildfowl of various kinds. There is a brief hunting season for pheasant in some Panhandle counties in December. Texans can hunt in their home counties without a license unless they are hunting deer or turkey. Texans under 17 and over 65 can get a certificate of exemption for a small fee. Everybody else requires a license. The fee is $5.25 for residents and more for people from out of the state.

1

2

3

2) The corn grows tall in the Panhandle sun and the farmers harvest it in October with combines. These machines cut the stalks, strip off the ears and remove the kernels from the cobs in one operation. Only clean corn is conveyed to the self-propelled carts traveling with the combines.

3) The carts shuttle between the combines and waiting trucks. They have their own conveyor system to transfer the grain. One diligent crew can harvest 50 acres of corn in a ten-hour day with these machines. Corn is the most expensive crop to grow here. Cotton requires more machinery but corn needs more water and more fertilizer. Most of the corn is fed to cattle.

1

1) Harvest time for the other grains is planting time for the Panhandle wheat. Most of the wheat grown here is winter wheat. It goes in the ground in the fall and it comes up but it does not begin growing until Spring. It is harvested in June and July.

2) The harvesting of wheat was one of the first big farm chores to be mechanized. Obed Hussey patented the first successful reaper in 1831. Cyrus McCormick got his patent in 1834. So harvesting machines were in use before the first wheat crop was planted on the Texas Plains. The early threshers were driven by steam.

3) Today's big combines are powered by diesel engines and they require far less manpower. Many farmers operate their machines themselves and hire little help.

2

3

1

1) Cotton is the top crop on the Plains. Growing cotton is a thoroughly mechanized business, now. But the machinery was a long time being perfected. There was some unfavorable reaction when the first cotton was planted here because it still had to be picked by hand then and oldtimers on the Plains did not want to share their world with cotton pickers. But migrant workers did the harvesting the first few years.

2) The cotton bolls are open by late Fall and the cotton is ready to be harvested. Farmers may have their fields sprayed with chemicals to kill the foliage or they may wait for the cold weather to kill it.

3) But they don't bring the harvesting machines into the fields until the foliage is all dead. The machines strip the plants and collect the cotton in the cages.

3

2

1) Cotton farmers have been delivering their cotton to the gins in trailers like these for many years.

2) The gins are equipped with vacuum systems that suck the cotton up and blow it into the machines that clean it and remove the seeds.

3) But this system is giving way to a more efficient and more expensive system of delivering the crop from the field to the gin. Many Plains farmers have bought hydraulic compacting machines called module builders. These are parked in the fields and filled with cotton. The hydraulic machinery packs the cotton tight. The compacted module is left standing in the field and the module builder is moved to another spot to repeat the process.

3

1

1) It would take a lot of trailers to haul this much cotton to the gin. A module may contain ten tons of cotton. Stems and trash are compacted with the cotton and they help give the modules some rigidity. They may be covered if they are going to be left in the field any length of time. But the modules are so tightly packed they will hold their shape in the Panhandle winds and they hang together while the special trucks from the gin are picking them up. This truck has a row of conveyor belts in the bed. The operator can back up to a module, tilt the bed, turn on the conveyors, take the module aboard and be on his way in a couple of minutes without getting out of the cab. Most of the old barbed wire fences have been removed from the big cotton and grain farms on the Plains — to allow the machines room to maneuver.

2) The ordinary vacuum system will not pick up this compacted cotton — so the gins are adding another new piece of machinery. This automatic feeder chews into the compacted module and conveys the cotton to the machines inside the gin.

2

1

2

1) The machinery inside the gins has not changed as much recently as the machinery involved in getting the cotton here. The gins remove all the trash and seeds and put the clean cotton up in bales.

2) A conveyor belt pushes the bagged and banded bales out onto the loading platform where the farmers claim them. The gins usually keep the seeds. The seeds usually pay the cost of ginning. The cotton goes from the gin to the nearest compress where government inspectors grade it. There are 29 grades and nine fiber lengths. There is no "fair-to-middling" grade. That is just a slang expression.

3) This is the machinery required just to harvest cotton.

3

1) A deluxe model cotton harvester can cost as much as $48,500. The fancier models deliver cleaner cotton. This reduces the cost of ginning so there is more than vanity involved in choosing models.

2) A good combine can cost nearly $90,000. But a combine can be used to harvest wheat and corn and sorghum. A cotton harvester is used only a few days a year unless it is owned by a contractor doing harvesting for others. Some Plains farmers have their harvesting done by contractors. Most prefer to have their own machines.

1

2

3

3) Big farms need big tractors and big tractors run up the farmer's overhead in a hurry. This unit retails for about $80,000. Some models are more expensive. The tax depreciation schedules encourage it and farmers are inclined to invest in expensive machinery when they are making money. Quite small towns on the Plains may have three or four equipment dealers. They do well when the farmers are doing well and they suffer when the farmers are suffering. These new tractors and combines and harvesters come with air conditioning and two-way radios and some of them have stereo.

1

1) Several vegetables do well on the Plains with irrigation. Carrots, onions, potatoes and peppers are the most popular. This is a mechanical carrot harvester at work in Deaf Smith County. More Plains farmers are experimenting with grapes, too.

2) Sunflowers do well here. This variety produces cooking oil and stock feed. The flowers with the seeds people eat are another variety.

3) Substantial crops of sugar beets are grown in Deaf Smith County, which also has a big sugar mill.

3

2

Plains farmers worry that they may have to quit using the underground water, even before it runs out, because of the cost of operating pumps. Natural gas was very cheap when the farmers started using it in their pump engines. It is very expensive now and likely to get more expensive and electricity is not cheap, either. H. L. Ayers may have the answer. He grows cotton and wheat on his farm at Crowell in Foard County. He installed two wind generators in 1981. They furnish electricity for his house and for his irrigation pumps when the wind is blowing at a decent rate. Ayers has a deal with the power company that lets him buy electricity from the company when his generators are not producing enough. The company buys electricity from him when the generators are producing a surplus.

This is another view of the weathering formation pictured on the cover. It is a fragment of the Cap Rock in Tule Canyon in Briscoe County. It is on private property but right on State Highway 207 just below Mackenzie Reservoir.

Index

Bold type represents the location of a related photograph.

Cator, Bob: 147
Cator, James H.: 146
Cator's Zulu Stockade: 147
Cattle raising: 167, **167**
C. B. Livestock Company: 56
Callahan Divide: 2
Campbell, H. H.: 35
Cattle branding: 77
Castro County: 81
Castro County Courthouse: **82**
Castro County Historical Museum: **83**
Castro, Henri: 81, 82
Channing: 157, **159**
Cheyennes: 113, 137
Chicago, Rock Island and Gulf Railroad:
    106, 138, 150, 151
Chickamauga: 63
Childress: 40
Childress County: 40
Childress County Courthouse: **41**
Childress County Heritage Museum: **41**
Childress, George Campbell: 40
Chittenden, Larry: 14
Clairemont: 22, **22**
Clarendon: 118, 119
Clarendon College: **119**
Claude: **115**, 117,
Cochran County: 68
Cochran County Courthouse: **69**
Cochran County Museum: **69**
Cochran, Robert: 69
Codman: 135
Coldwater: 150, 151, **151**
Coldwater Creek: 149
Coleman, L. G.: 37
Coleman Park, Brownfield: 65
Coleto Creek: 18
Collingsworth County: 119
Collingsworth County Courthouse: **121**
Collingsworth County Historical Museum:
    121
Collingsworth County Pioneers' Park: **121**
Collinsworth, James: 119
Colorado River: 2
Colton, Walter: 151
Comancheros: 83, 89
Comanches: 8, 17, 22, 24, 32, 61, 83, 84,
    89, 92, 111, 122, 125, 126, 137, 142
Conner, L. G.: 113
Connor, W. G.: 84
Convention of 1836: 41, 102
Copper Breaks State Park: **44**
Coronado: 130
Cos, Martin Perfecto de: 85
Cottle County: 33
Cottle County Courthouse: **34**
Cottle, George Washington: 33
Cotton: 171, **171**, 172, **172**, 173, **173**, 174,
    174
Cowboys' Christmas Ball: 14
Cox, Paris: 54
Cree's Tree: **141**
Criswell, W. H.: 134
Crosby County: 54

Crosby County Courthouse: **56**
Crosby, Stephen: **55**, 57
Crosbyton: 54
Curry Comb Ranch: 57
CV Ranch: 34

D
Dalhart: 157
Dallam County: 157
Dallam County Courthouse: **162**
Dallam, James Wilmer: 162
Darrouzett: 129
Dary, Dave: 122
Daugherty house, Brownfield: **65**
Daughters of the Republic of Texas: 94
Davis, Jefferson: 107
Deaf Smith County: 107
Deaf Smith County Courthouse: **108**
Deaf Smith County Historical Museum:
    109
Declaration of Independence: 35, 41, 43,
    79, 85, 94, 102, 120, 134, 142
Della Plain: 90
Denver City: 66
Dickens: 25
Dickens County: 23
Dickens County Courthouse: **25**
Dickerson, John and Wiley: 121
Dimmit: 82-83
Dimmit, W. C.: 82
Ding Dong Daddy: 156
Don Harrington Discovery Center: **102**
Donley County: 117
Donley County Courthouse: **118**
Donley, Stockton P.: 117
Double Lakes: 61
Double U Company: 59
Dumas: 156
Dumas, Louis: **153**, 156
Duncan, Arthur: 90
Duval, Burr: 18
Dyess Air Force Base: **3**

E
Edwards, Benjamin: 79
Edwards, C. O.: 62
Edwards Plateau: 2
Eighth Texas Cavalry: 53, 63
Elliot, Margaret A. Museum, Spur: **24**
Ellis, Richard: 41
Ellwood, I. L.: **71**
Emma: 56
Epworth: 86
Estacado: **55**, 56
Estelline: **38**
Exell Helium Plant: **155**

F
Fannin, James: 18
Farnsworth: 132
Farwell: 148

Hurley, Patrick J: 76
Hutchinson, Anderson: 146
Hutchinson County: 142
Hutchinson County Courthouse: **143**
Hutchinson County Museum: **143**

I
INDEPENDENCE: 11
INVINCIBLE: 11
IOA Ranch: 48
Irrigation: 86, 87, 88, 168, **168**

J
JA Ranch: 84, 93, 113, 114, **116**
Jackson, Stonewall: 20, **20**
Jayton: 21
Jennings, Waylon: 74
Jones City: 14
Jones County: 13
Jones County Courthouse: **15**
Jones, Anson: 13
Jones and Plummer Trail: 131

K
Kent, Andrew: 23
Kent County: 21
Kent County Courthouse: **23**
King County: 26
King County Courthouse: **26**
King, William P.: 26
Kiowas: 8, 17, 24, 61, 113, 126, 137, 142
Knight, Tom: 9
Knox City: 29
Knox County: 28
Knox County Courthouse: **29**
Knox, Henry: 28

L
Lake Abilene: **2**
Lake Fort Phantom Hill: **14**
Lake Marvin: **128**
Lake McClellan: **139**
Lake Meredith: **143, 155**
Lamar, Mirabeau: 53, 153
Lamb County: 73
Lamb County Courthouse: **74**
Lamb, George A.: 73
*LAND OF THE UNDERGROUND
   RAIN:* 87
Landergrin, John: 106
Landergrin, P. H.: 106
Last Frontier Rodeo: 68
Lawrence, B. L.: 18
Lefors, Pierre: 138
Lehman: 69
Lester house, Canyon: 111
Levelland: 72
LIBERTY: 11
Lipscomb: 129
Lipscomb, Abner S.: 129

Lipscomb County: 129
Lipscomb County Courthouse: **129**
Littlefield: 75
Littlefield City Park: **74**
Littlefield Lands Company: 75
Littlefield, George W.: 71, 74, **74**, 76
Lockney: 90
Lockney Christian College: 90
Loco: 42
LONE STAR: 32
Lone Wolf: 144
Lowe, E. L.: 87
Lubbock: 48, 51
Lubbock Christian College: **49**
Lubbock Civic Center: **50**
Lubbock County: 48
Lubbock County Courthouse: **50**
Lubbock Lake Archaeological Site: **48**
Lubbock, Thomas S.: 51, 63
LX Ranch: 103
Lyman Wagon Train Battle Site: **126**
Lynn County: 61
Lynn County Courthouse: 61
Lynn, W.: 62

M
Mackenzie, Ranald: 22, 24, 43, 61, 84, 89,
   92, 110, 122, 125, 137
Mackenzie Reservoir: **94**
Mackenzie State Park: **52**
Magee, Augustus W.: 38
Madame Queen steam engine: **101**
Magruder, John: 137
Mallet Ranch: 71
Marcy, Randolph: 17, 198
Margaret: 31, **31,** 45
Marietta: 55
Marsh, Stanley: 104
Matador: 36
Matador Ranch: 24, 35, **36**
Masterson, Bat: **146**
Maxwell, Z. T.: 87
McAdams, J. J.: 34
McAdoo: 23
McClellan Creek: 137
McClellan, George: **44**
McCormick, Frenchy: 106
McCormick, Mickey: 106
McMurry College: 4
Medicine Lodge Treaty: 8
Medicine Mound: **44**
Memphis: 37
Merchant, John: 13
Miami: 134-136
Miles, Nelson: 126
Mobeetie: 123
Mobeetie Museum: **123**
Monterrey: 151
Moody Hotel, Canadian: **127**
Moore County Courthouse: **154**
Moore County Historical Museum: **154**
Moore, Edwin W.: 153
Morton: 68

Photo Credits:

The photographs for this book were made by Ray Miller, Gary James, Bill Springer, Mark Williams, Bob Brandon, John Treadgold and Fred Edison, with the exception of those listed below. The author and the publisher wish to express their gratitude to these individuals and organizations for permitting the reproduction of photographs from their collections.

The first number indicates the page, the number in parentheses is the number of the picture on the page.

DALHART TEXAN: 163 (1), 164 (1)

HISTORY OF LIPSCOMB COUNTY: 95, 130 (2)

Houston Public Library: 39 (1), 43 (1), 44 (4), 64 (1), 67 (1), 71 (3), 74 (1), 92 (1), 99 (1), 108 (1), 111 (3), 120, 128 (4), 136 (1), 137, 146, 150 (2)

Panhandle-Plains Historical Museum, Canyon: 158 (2), 166

Texas A&M (James Vance): 170 (3)

TEXAS HIGHWAYS: 16 (2)

Texas Parks and Wildlife Department: 156, 169 (1)

U.S. Air Force: 3 (2)

Will Rogers Memorial, Claremore, Oklahoma: 130 (1)

XIT Museum, Dalhart: 163 (1)

XIT RANCH OF TEXAS, Haley, and Nita Stewart Haley Museum, Midland: 79 (1), 159 (1)

Acknowledgements:

We are indebted to Doris Glasser and the staff of the Texas Room of the Houston Public Library, to the Texas State Library in Austin, to the Institute of Texas Cultures in San Antonio and to the Panhandle Plains Museum in Canyon for assisting us in our research.

Some of the publications we found helpful and worthy of recommendation to readers wishing more information are:

"Handbook of Texas," Vols. I, II, III; "Texas Almanac, 1980"; "Texas, Land of Contrast"; "Why Stop?"; "The National Register of Historic Places in Texas"; "Texas Museum Directory"; "Guide to Official Texas Historical Markers"; "Old Texas Trails" by Williams; "Lone Star" by Fehrenbach; "The Buffalo Book" by Dary; "Thirty Years of Army Life on the Border" by Marcy; "The History of Lipscomb County"; "The Republic of Texas" by Jones, "Between Sun and Sod" by Lewis; "Land of the Underground Rain" by Green; "XIT Ranch of Texas" by Haley; "A Collection of Memories" by Armstrong County Historical Association; "Old Ranches of the Texas Plains" by Rogers and Wilder; "Amarillo" by Hammond.